Becoming Mama

A FAITH-BASED JOURNEY INTO MOTHERHOOD

Jenni Helm

Ark House Press
arkhousepress.com

© 2025 Jenni Helm

All rights reserved. Apart from any fair dealing for the purpose of study, research, criticism, or review, as permitted under the Copyright Act, no part may be reproduced by any process without written permission.

Unless otherwise stated, all Scriptures are taken from the New International Translation (Holy Bible. Copyright© 1996, 2004, 2007, 2013 by Tyndale House Foundation. Used by permission of Tyndale House Publishers Inc., Carol Stream, Illinois 60188. All rights reserved.)

Some names and identifying details have been changed to protect the privacy of individuals.

Cataloguing in Publication Data:
Title: Becoming Mama
ISBN: 978-1-7641362-9-7 (pbk)
Subjects: REL012160 RELIGION / Christian Living / Parenting; FAM025000 FAMILY & RELATIONSHIPS / Life Stages / Infants & Toddlers; HEA041000   HEALTH & FITNESS / Pregnancy & Childbirth.

Design by initiateagency.com

I dedicate this book to Abba Father creator
of everything, and loving Papa.
King Jesus, Saviour, Messiah and Provider
Holy Spirit Comforter, Guide and Partner.

Thanks to
To my daughter, Kelsie and my precious granddaughter Gracie
who have shared their photos and have journeyed
with me on this path together recently.
Jack for always being so encouraging and
taught me so much about myself.
Laura and Brandon Zoing for sharing their
personal photos of their journey.
Nellie Jamison who has tirelessly edited this book.
To all my friends for their support.

Children are God's love-gift; they are heaven's generous reward.
Psalms 127:3

TABLE OF CONTENTS

Chapter 1- Listening to God 1

Chapter 2- Finding your Peace 15

Chapter 3- God's character 25

Chapter 4- Values and Vision 35

Chapter 5- Practical steps for pregnancy 43

Chapter 6- Establishing a support network- Finding your Village 59

Chapter 7- Breastfeeding 69

Chapter 8- Understanding Emotional Regulation 85

Chapter 9- What makes a positive birthing experience? 102

Chapter 10- Baby Cues and Sleep 115

Chapter 11- The New You 129

Chapter 12- The Fourth Trimester 147

AUTHOR BIO - JENNI HELM

Jenni Helm is a devoted Child and Family Health Nurse, Midwife, and International Board Certified Lactation Consultant (IBCLC) who has spent her career walking alongside women and families in the sacred early years of parenting. With over three decades of experience, she is known for her compassionate, strengths-based approach, empowering mothers to make informed choices that align with their values, culture, and intuition.

Jenni is the founder of *Learning the Baby Dance*, a heart-led initiative offering parent support, education, and community groups often run in partnership with her local church. Deeply rooted in her Christian faith, Jenni believes that we live out our full purpose when we walk each step with Jesus, and this belief infuses every aspect of her work with hope and grace.

She holds a Masters Child and Family Health and has held specialist clinical roles in both Midwifery and Child Health across hospital and community settings, including work with Indigenous families. Jenni is passionate about improving long-term health outcomes by promoting and supporting mothers, always trusting the wisdom of a mother's heart that is God given.

Her most cherished role, however, has been raising her children, Kelsie and Jack. She is now Grammy to the beautiful Grace—her greatest joy.

This book has been led by God each step of the way. Jenni prays it will help you enter Motherhood with grace, confidence and purpose.

INTRODUCTION

Are you pregnant and excited but also a bit nervous about how you will manage your new role as mum? We have all been there. I remember being hit with the reality and the enormity of this new role as I gazed into the eyes of my newborn baby Kelsie. I looked at her and thought "How can I do this? She is so precious. What if I make a mess of her life?" I then looked up to God and asked for His help. He never let me down. It's like nothing you have ever experienced before. We all have developed ways to manage life and feel in control. This is turned on its head when you have a baby as there are many things you can't control and oh, the emotions! If we can learn to release our control and place the journey into God's hands it will be a smoother, more peaceful time. Motherhood was never meant to be done on our own. Thankfully God walks with us every step of the way. He does not want to be the silent partner but wants to give you love, guidance and direction every day. Mostly he wants to love you. You need to know how much He loves you.

Do you wonder what sort of mum you will be? We often have a mental image of what we want to be like. To be a calm loving mother we may need to do some work on ourselves a bit. I remember wanting to be a calm loving mum. I constantly let myself and my children down by raising my voice and letting my emotions get away with me. I had not understood how to remain calm in the craziness. I did not know how to listen to God's promptings. I did not fully trust God's purpose for me in this journey. Don't misunderstand, I was a calm loving mum most of the time. I prayed a lot! I had some work to do to understand me and my emotions. Back then we did not understand emotional regulation as much as we do now. In many ways I was still the little girl was lost when I lost my mum at 18 years.

The first thing I will say, learn how to be kind to yourself. We are often so critical of ourselves, and God does not want that. To care for your baby, you need to look after yourself with gentleness, so you can care for your baby out of fullness, not lack. Remember the little girl inside you who needs love and care. Look after her with the passion that you have inside you, to look after your child. We often look to those around us to fill our cup emotionally. If you can learn to go to God for that, you will not need to seek from others what they cannot give.

Proverbs 4:23 (TPT)
"So above all, guard the affections of your heart,
for they affect all that you are.
Pay attention to the welfare of your innermost being,
for from there flows the wellspring of life."

This book is designed to walk you through the process of preparing for your baby emotionally and spiritually with the help of Jesus.

INTRODUCTION

Listen to the song "Imago Dei" by Sean Feucht.

Before I was formed
I was loved and adored by a father
Who knows me by name
You sewed me together
And buried Your treasure
Inside of a soul and a frame

Imago Dei
I'm fearfully, wonderfully made
Imago Dei
There's glory in all You create

Before my conception
My home was in heaven
And You breathed Your life in my lungs
Your perfect design
That You purposed in time
Wholly made in the image of God
I am made in the image of God

Imago Dei
I'm fearfully, wonderfully made
Imago Dei
There's glory in all You create

Oh what a miracle, fully intentional
All that You fashion, it is good
Isn't it obvious, not a coincidence
Life is Your passion, it is good
Oh what a miracle, fully intentional
All that You fashion, it is good
Isn't it obvious, not a coincidence
Life is Your passion, it is good

> Imago Dei
> I'm fearfully, wonderfully made
> Imago Dei
> There's glory in all You create

Before we start let's pray

Heavenly Father, I come before You with an open heart as I begin this journey of preparing for this little one You've entrusted to me. I invite Your presence and ask for Your guidance. Help me to hear Your voice clearly, understand Your direction, and walk into this calling with the grace You have given me. I trust that You will lead this process and have beautiful plans beyond what I can imagine. I choose to submit to You in caring for this child. Give me the strength to make good choices for them.

Thank You for drawing me closer to You through this season. Show me the healing I need for this journey.

In Jesus' name,

Amen.

Let me take you on a journey. I want you to still your mind and body.

Matthew 6:6 (MSG)
"Here's what I want you to do: Find a quiet, secluded place so you won't be tempted to role-play before God. Just be there as simply and honestly as you can manage. The focus will shift from you to God, and you will begin to sense His grace."

INTRODUCTION

Listen and feel the life inside you. Right there inside you is one of God's miracles. Put your hand on your belly. Tell your child how much you are looking forward to meeting them. This is a precious child being created in the secret place. Trust God's process.

Psalms 139:13, 15, 16 (TPT)
"You formed my innermost being, shaping my delicate inside and my intricate outside and wove them all together in my mother's womb. You even formed every bone in my body when you created me in the secret place; carefully, skilfully you shaped me from nothing to something. You saw who you created me to be before I became me!"

Pray through this over them.

> *Precious child it doesn't matter about how you were conceived; you were planned by God to come into this world for this time. God has given you to me as your mother, to teach, counsel and comfort. May He show me how to do this each day. May He guide you also as you grow and develop inside me and every minute of your life how ever long that will be. May He be the centre of your life forever.*
>
> *In Jesus Name, Amen*

Believe that just as God created the world, He can guide you through this pregnancy.

The internet is wonderful but, in many ways, it has made pregnancy more stressful. I love that mothers can find information for themselves, but it is sometimes difficult to discern truth from fiction, and it can be very confusing. I pray that this journey will help you to follow Jesus' footsteps.

Let's begin!

CHAPTER 1
Listening to God

Jeremiah 33:3
"Call to Me and I will answer you.
I will tell you marvellous and wondrous things that you could never figure out on your own."

I was born into a Christian family. My father was a Baptist minister. I knew about God from when I was a little child. I made my first decision for God at 9 years of age. I was taught good biblical grounding, but I was not taught how to listen to His whispers. Earlier this year I did Roma Waterman's 5-day prophetic plan online. It was what I needed to lean into Jesus more. This book came out of that time spent seeking what God wanted me to put my efforts into now. It has brought all my experience and training together, but it was written leaning into God's whispers. God wants us to hear His voice. I responded to God telling me He was real and loved me deeply again when I was 16 years old. I heard His whisper. Why do so many Christians then live without leaning into what He is saying to us? He is reaching out all the time. Are we listening? Knowing our value in God and how much He loves us will change everything. It's not just head knowledge. It is an intimate relationship with Jesus. It is in the conversations we have with Him where we find true relationship. I wish I had this information as a young mother raising two children without my mother.

You were handpicked to be this child's mother. How amazing is that! God does not expect you to be perfect and you will need His help. We often think that the responsibility is all on our shoulders. God is so invested in your child. He expects you to need His guidance. Being a mother will stretch you in ways that you don't expect. You will change in so many ways. Research has confirmed that our brain changes, our life definitely does. You will have to reach deeply into your very soul. Know that no other person will know your child like you will. God has given you a deep knowing about your baby. Just as nothing takes Him by surprise about you, nothing will catch Him off guard about your baby.

Psalms 139:1 (TPT)
"Lord, You know everything there is to know about me."

We as parents will find peace and wisdom when we seek God with intention in our decisions, drawing on Him, our God, for guidance day to day, minute by minute.

James 1:5 (TPT)
"And if anyone longs to be wise, ask God for wisdom and He will give it! He won't see your lack of wisdom as an opportunity to scold you over your failures, but He will overwhelm your failures with His generous grace."

We are all human and as such will make mistakes. Thank God for His love for you and your child. He will guide you if you just listen. We are made in God's image and when we are growing a precious child of God, we are very close to His heart.

Trust your God given intuition with this child. God gave you this child to care for and he will prompt you when you need to act. Learn to be able to discern when to accept or reject what others may say in this journey. Go to God with everything.

God is Transcendent. Transcendence means God is above and beyond everything we know. He *excels and surpasses all known things, going beyond usual limits.*

God is also Immanent. Immanence is the quality of being contained within, or remaining within the boundaries of a person, of the world, or of the mind. In other words, the ability for us to enjoy intimate relationship with God.

> *Psalm 33:4-5 (NLT)*
> *"For the Word of the Lord holds true,*
> *and we can trust everything He does.*
> *He loves whatever is just and good;*
> *the unfailing love of the Lord fills the earth."*

How can you prepare for this amazing work you are about to do?

We are going to explore where God needs to take you to prepare you. This journey will look different for everyone.

Proverbs 3:5 (TPT)
"Trust in the Lord completely,
and do not rely on your own opinions.
With all your heart rely on Him to guide you,
and He will lead you in every decision you make."

John 10:27 (ESV)
"My sheep hear My voice;
I know them, and they follow Me."

As a mother there will be times you will feel overwhelmed. Ask Him for strategies. Ask Him who to call for advice. You might be thinking.... how do I hear God? God promises He will lead you and speak to you. You might be thinking you can't hear God's voice, He is speaking all the time. Sometimes we are just too busy with too many things taking our attention. We need to be intentional to hear His voice. We need to stop and listen.

It's a bit like an old-fashioned radio; you need to turn it on and tune it in to the station. We need to set aside time to sit with Him and tune out distractions so we can hear Him. We can be distracted by so many other things that make it hard for us to hear Him.

Psalm 46:10-11 (TPT)
"Surrender your anxiety.
Be still and realize that I am God.
I am God above all the nations,
and I am exalted throughout the whole earth.
Here He stands! The Commander!

The mighty Lord of Angel Armies is on our side!
The God of Jacob fights for us!
Pause in His presence"

HOW GOD SPEAKS TO US

Have you ever wondered how God speaks to us? He communicates in many ways, and when we learn to recognize His voice, we can grow closer to Him. He is always speaking to us.

Here are some ways He speaks:

Scripture

The Bible is the primary way God speaks to us, it is His living Word. As you spend time in Scripture, you will get to know His voice. He may bring a specific verse to mind. When this happens, look it up and ask, *"Jesus, what are You telling me?"* Write it down, read different translations, underline key words, and explore their meanings. The words of a verse may jump off the page at you.

Isaiah 30:21
Your ears shall hear a word behind you, saying,
"This is the way, walk in it,
whenever you turn to the right hand
or whenever you turn to the left."

Songs

Ever wake up with a song stuck in your head that won't go away? God often speaks through music. He actually sings over us.

> *Zephaniah 3:17 NKJV*
> *"The Lord your God in your midst,*
> *The Mighty One, will save:*
> *He will rejoice over you with gladness,*
> *He will quiet you with His love,*
> *He will rejoice over you with singing"*

A song might play on social media or come to you unexpectedly, carrying a message from Him. Music has the power to draw us into His presence. I once had a friend send me the song *Psalm 23* at a moment when I needed it most. She had no idea what I was going through, but she felt prompted to share it and it was like a love letter from God.

Circumstances

God can use everyday situations to reveal truth to us. I once attended a work in-service while facing a difficult season in my life. As I listened, I suddenly realized that what was being described was exactly what I was experiencing. It was a lightbulb moment! God was giving me clarity about the decisions I needed to make.

I remember cleaning up a broken vase one day which the wind had knocked over. As I picked up the tiny pieces, a phrase came to mind: *"Wisdom knows when something is broken beyond repair."* Instantly, I knew what God was telling me.

Words & Repetition

Sometimes, God highlights a specific word or phrase that keeps appearing in books, Scripture, conversations, or even on a bumper sticker. A friend or family member might unknowingly confirm something God had already been speaking to your heart.

Lessons from Everyday Life

God can also speak through the things we experience. Once, I was trying to catch my rescue horse. She loved being with me but would circle just out of reach, unsure if she could fully trust me. I asked God, *"Why does she do this?"* His response was gentle but clear: *"She is just like you. You hover close but hesitate to come fully to Me. I am safe, and you love being with Me when you allow yourself to be in My presence."* That truth impacted me deeply.

Dreams

Throughout scriptures God speaks through our dreams. Creativity sometimes comes in dreams, Inventions like the sewing machine, google, theory of relativity, the song "Imagine" by John Lennon, all came from dreams. Ask God what the dream means and what He is saying to you. Write it down so you don't forget. Sometimes complete meaning comes later.

Job 33:14,15
"For God does speak—now one way,
now another, though no one perceives it.
In a dream, in a vision of the night,
when deep sleep falls on people as they slumber in their beds"

> *Genesis 46;2*
> *"And God spoke to Israel in a vision at night and said,*
> *"Jacob! Jacob!" "Here I am," he replied."*

> *Acts 16 :9*
> *"During the night Paul had a vision of a man of Macedonia*
> *standing and begging him,*
> *"Come over to Macedonia and help us.""*

Roma Waterman states in her book "The Prophetic Plan" Your dreams are connected to your destiny. So why do we have dreams from God? "They reveal what's going on in your heart, bypassing the normal filters that you would normally have in your rational mind."

Adam Thomas from the book "The Divinity Code." "They build courage, give direction, bring conviction and correction."

Caroline Leaf states in her book "Switch on your Brain" "At night when you sleep, your thinking gets sorted out".

Neurogenesis is the birth of new baby nerve cells that are born as we sleep. This is how we process emotions and find solutions to our problems. If I can't work something out strategically, I give it to God, I sleep on it and He gives me an idea, it happens when I'm sleeping, or He wakes me in the quiet of the early hours.

> Strategies in dreams- (Roma Waterman)
>
> 1/Write it down as soon as you wake. Lord did you give me a dream? Is it for me or for someone else? Any colours in the dream? Numbers also matter.

2/ Are there any scriptures I can attach to this dream?

3/ What are you trying to say God? What is this dream about? Is it about correction or the future?

4/ How did you feel when you woke up?

Repeated dreams are God trying to get your attention.

HOW CAN WE BE SURE IT'S GOD?

God will never contradict His Scripture. God's words illuminate things as He is light. His words bring light, peace, and encouragement, even when He corrects us. His voice brings clarity to your thoughts and situation. We will feel safe.

If you're unsure whether something is from God, sit with it. Pray and ask Him to confirm it. Search Scripture, and trust that He will make His voice known to you. I will often say to God; "If this is you, keep reminding me about it." Search out scripture that confirm what you have heard. Ask someone you trust to pray about it.

Satan's words will make you doubt God or yourself. It will feel uncomfortable and cause more stress. You will be more confused.

John 10:10 TPT
"The thief's purpose is to steal and kill and destroy.
My purpose is to give them a rich and satisfying life."

I was listening to a podcast with Roma Waterman and Youth Pastor Sarah Camez, she said the voice is usually one of 3 voices.

1/ Satan's voice will confuse, cause us to doubt or do something we know in our heart is wrong. It will conflict with scripture or a perversion of it. It will be hypercritical. I'm so stupid. Why is she wearing that? Satan's words will make you doubt God or yourself. The enemy's words bring confusion, stress, and fear.

2/ It will be our voice. This sounds like I'm cold, I need to get up and go, I'm hungry. Our mind is usually self-focused.

3/ It will be God's voice. Encouraging, motivating, confirming scripture. As I said before it will feel safe. God's voice is restorative, may be challenging. Pray for that lady on the bus stop. Go here this person needs you. He is kind and truthful. He will never speak out of character.

This next excerpt is taken from Roma Waterman's book "The Prophetic Plan"

Practice the Art of Listening

Here is the next portion of today's exercise. Find a quiet moment (even in a noisy place) and practice being still internally. Close your eyes and become aware of the sounds around you. Then, go deeper and ask, "What can I hear with my spiritual ears? What is the Lord trying to say?"

This comes from a beautiful book called *The Creative Call* by Janice Elsheimer. It's a way to investigate how you hear and sense things. You might be surprised at what you start to notice when you really tune in.

So find a quiet place inside of yourself—get quiet on the inside. You might even go to a cafe or live on a busy road, but I want to encourage you; it doesn't matter because what we're trying to do is bring the stillness of the Lord, into our hearts. I want you to sit somewhere comfortably and take a deep breath.

Now, close your eyes and be aware of the sounds around you. Think about the sounds you are hearing. You may listen to the cars rushing by. You may hear the kids play in the background. You may hear the whir of an air conditioner, rain, or trees moving in the wind.

Pause and just take in every single sound. What you will find when you do this is that you will start to notice sounds you didn't even know were there. I remember the first time I did this; I could hear a creaking sound in my chair that I didn't even know existed because I was honing in and going deeper into what I could listen to.

> Now, once you have started to hear all the sounds around you, ask yourself this question: "What can I hear with my spiritual ears? What am I hearing in the spirit?" And then, as you pause to listen to that which is hidden behind the quiet, ask this question: "Lord, what do you want to say?"
>
> Roma Waterman

When you first stop to listen, it will be hard. You may need to put on worship music or may need the help of a bible meditation. You may find yourself distracted. Be kind to yourself and just bring yourself back to the task. Closing your eyes can help.

2 Corinthians 12:9-11
"My grace is sufficient for you,
for My power is made perfect in weakness."

Isaiah 40:11 (NKJV)
"He will feed His flock like a shepherd;
He will gather the lambs with His arm,
And carry them in His bosom,
And gently lead those who are with young."

Lectio Divina is another way to listen to God

It is a way of praying the scriptures that leads us deeper into God's word. We slow down. We read a short passage more than once. We chew it over slowly and carefully. We savour it. Scripture begins to speak to us in a new way. It speaks to us personally and aids that union we have with God through Christ who is Himself the Living Word.

Psalm 46:10
"Be still and know that I am God, I will be exalted among the nations, among the earth. The Lord Almighty is with us; the God of Jacob is our fortress"

Lectio (Read) – Slowly and prayerfully read the passage, Listening for a word, phrase or image that stands out.

Posture: Receiving the text.

Meditatio (Meditate/ Reflect) – Turn that word or phrase over in your heart. What might God be saying to you through it?

Posture: Pondering and personalising.

Oratio (Pray / Respond) – Respond to God in prayer about what you've heard. This could be praise, confession, petition or gratitude.

Posture: Dialogue with God.

Contemplatio (Contemplate / Rest) – Move beyond words into silence, resting in God's presence. Simply be with him.

Posture: Abiding and resting.

REFERENCES:

Roma Waterman 2024 The Prophetic plan Published by: I Was Carried Pty Ltd

Distributed by: I Was Carried Pty Ltd

HeartSong Youth - 3 Steps to Hearing God's Voice as a teen: Meet the HeartSong Youth Leaders!

https://www.youtube.com/watch?v=2nOjnVkHIok&t=1838s

Elsheimer, Janice. 2009. *The Creative Call: An Artist's Response to the Way of the Spirit.* 1st ed. Colorado Springs: WaterBrook & Multnomah.

Roma Waterman's explanation of Lectio Divina from 4 day plan Chaos to Calm 2025.

CHAPTER 2

Finding your Peace

John 14:27 "Peace I leave with you;
My peace I give you.
I do not give to you as the world gives."

Babies learn so much in the early years. The biggest thing they learn is Trust vs Mistrust. It takes courage to let your child see into you but without intimacy they will not learn to trust. What do we do when we are ashamed of ourselves or something we have experienced? Without knowing we shut ourselves off to people we love, our children, our partner and our God. We build walls to protect ourselves, not knowing that this makes our life less.

Intimacy- into me you see. This is a process of babies feeling safe, being able to be vulnerable and being totally accepted. This is how a baby can learn to trust. We need to be open for this to happen.

> Danny Silk – School of Faith explains it this way
>
> "I think a lot of us learn to not trust from our experiences in childhood. A lot of us learn that it's not a safe place, that the parents in authority cannot handle the truth. They cannot handle what's going on with my life. They need me to give them what they want. They need me to show them what they want to see. They cannot handle what's going on with me and therefore I can't be me, I can't show me. I can't show you me because it will overload your circuit. It will take you beyond what you can handle and you're going to get scared by what's going on inside of me, because you would never let what's going on in me, go inside you or it's going to derail you. We are practising how vulnerable and how true we can be and if my parents don't know how to do intimacy and they don't know how to do intimacy in their marriage and they don't know how to live vulnerably, they're going to train me in that."

Psalm 32:8 (TPT)
"I hear the Lord saying, "I will stay close to you,
instructing and guiding you along the pathway for your life.
I will advise you along the way and lead you
forth with My eyes as your guide."

FINDING OUR PEACE: PREPARING FOR MOTHERHOOD WITH A RESTED HEART

This chapter is so important. I felt God truly wanted it in this book because peace is foundational to entering pregnancy and motherhood with confidence and strength. The more peace you carry into this journey, the more you can be fully present with your baby. But finding that peace may require making peace with your past. We all have things we need to release to Jesus.

We come from different families, carrying experiences that shape us. Some of those experiences will be beautiful and life-giving, while others may be painful or even traumatic. Now is the time to reflect, to consciously decide what you will bring into your role as a mother and what you will choose to leave behind.

Your baby will feel your peace just as much as they would feel your stress. This doesn't mean you have to be perfect or have everything figured out. It simply means inviting God into your heart, allowing Him to heal what needs healing, and trusting Him to guide you.

If looking back is too painful, you don't have to do it alone. Seeking support, whether through prayer, trusted friends, or a counsellor can help you process and release what weighs you down.

God never intended for you to carry burdens that He can release. Peace isn't something we create on our own but it's something we receive. God's peace passes understanding. We can be in the middle of a storm but be at peace because we trust our God.

True peace comes from knowing that God has already gone before you. He is in your past, your present, and your future. He knows what you've been through, and He knows the kind of mother you are becoming. When stress or fear rises, take a breath and turn to Him. Let God help you find your peace. Not just for yourself, but for your baby, for your home, and for the generations to come.

This next exercise is for you and your husband/partner to do separately, then for both of you to do together. It will bring light to where healing is needed. Spend some time in prayer and praise if you can before you start this process. Ask God to guide you.

FAMILY OF ORIGIN AND ITS IMPACT ON MOTHERHOOD

We will explore both yours and your partners family of origin.

Family of Origin

- What was your childhood like?
- What roles did your mother and father do?
- What are your views on discipline?
- What are your ideas on sharing care?

Your family of origin is the family unit that raised you and it plays a significant role in shaping your beliefs, behaviours, and emotional responses. This influence extends beyond childhood and into motherhood, impacting how you care for your baby, navigate challenges, and make parenting decisions. The way you were cared for as a child may influence how you instinctively respond to your baby's needs. If you grew up in a nurturing, responsive environment, you might feel confident trusting your instincts as a mother. If your caregivers were inconsistent, dismissive, harsh or abusive, you may struggle with self-doubt or feel disconnected from your intuition. Understanding your family's approach to parenting whether positive or challenging can help you consciously choose what to carry forward and what to change for your own children.

THE SCIENCE OF GENERATIONAL TRAUMA AND GOD'S HEALING POWER

Research has recognized that family trauma doesn't just shape emotions and behaviours, it can also change your DNA. Trauma experienced by previous generations can alter genetic expression, influencing stress responses, mental health, and even physical health in future generations. But here's the good news: Science also shows that healing, through new experiences, relationships, healing and faith, can help rewrite those patterns.

God is greater than generational trauma. No matter what has been passed down to you, you are not bound by it. Jesus came to set us free, to break every chain, and to give us new life. We are going to bring these things to God, our fears, our hurts, our family burdens, so that He can restore what has been broken and create something new through us.

BREAKING UNHEALTHY PATTERNS TO FOSTER SECURE ATTACHMENT

Attachment patterns are often passed down through generations. If your family of origin struggled with emotional connection, independence was overly emphasized, or comfort was withheld, you might feel unsure about responding to your baby's needs with closeness and reassurance.

The good news is that secure attachment is not about perfection, it's about being present, responsive, and repairing moments of disconnection. By consciously choosing to meet your baby's emotional and physical needs with warmth and consistency, you are creating a new foundation of trust and security. And when you invite God into your parenting, you gain wisdom, strength, and peace beyond your own understanding.

Recognizing the influence of your family of origin can be empowering rather than limiting. By reflecting on your experiences, seeking healing through Jesus, and surrounding yourself with a supportive community, you can embrace what served you well and gently release what doesn't align with the mother you want to be. You are not bound by your past. You are creating something new with your husband and your child. And that is powerful.

Family of origin- How can I move past it? When you think of your childhood what emotions does it bring up? Did you feel seen and understood? It may help to get a big piece of paper and write all these down or draw pictures. Sometimes when things happen before we as children can talk, we will not have words but may be able to draw pictures.

Making our peace with our past. Letting go of the past disappointments and hurt is possible. Circle the things written down that are good. We will use these later in another exercise. Cross out the hurtful things you don't want to bring to your family life. You may want to cut them out and burn them in a physical way of letting go. We will address these things in the lemon story later.

Forgiveness- Do you have some people you need to forgive? Forgiveness does not always mean reconciliation. Unforgiveness can eat us up inside and affect our present relationships.

"Circle of Security" is a parents group run to explore how to parent children when you have had a difficult upbringing. It is run regularly in many areas. "Shark Music" is the music we can hear when our childs cries or their behaviour triggers something from our past. "Being With and Shark Music"- Circle of Security International is a clip on youtube you can watch that explains it well. It's so good that once we recognise our shark music and submit it to God for healing its effects on us diminishes.

Philippians 3:13-15 (TPT)
"I don't depend on my own strength to accomplish this. However, I do have one compelling focus: I forget all of the past as I fasten my heart to the future instead. I run straight for the divine invitation of reaching the heavenly goal and gaining the victory prize through the anointing of Jesus. So let all who are fully mature have this same passion, and if anyone is not yet gripped by these desires, God will reveal it to them."

This passage calls us to let go of the past and focus on the future God has for us. It acknowledges that we can't do this in our strength, we need God's help. It's exciting that you can get rid of all that could hold you back! Then you can step into the bright future the Lord has prepared for you.

Roma Waterman recounts this story

The Lemon Story: A Lesson in Letting Go

Let me share what I call "the lemon story." Years ago, I was teaching a Bible college class. As students walked in, I handed each a large lemon and instructed them to hold it in their writing hand for the entire 90-minute class. They were not allowed to let go.

Eventually, I addressed their frustration by explaining how this exercise perfectly illustrates how unforgiveness affects our lives.

Like the lemon, unforgiveness:

- Occupies our hands, preventing us from grasping new opportunities.
- Can cause discomfort and pain the longer we hold on to it.
- Distracts us from what's truly important.

I loved seeing their faces when they realised that we can all so easily carry unforgiveness like those lemons, and we need to do something about that if we want to move forward in all He wants for us.

The Many Faces of Unforgiveness

So, what does unforgiveness look like? It doesn't always look like being angry at someone who has wronged you. Here are some other identifications of unforgiveness:
Resentment towards others who have hurt us;
Disappointment in ourselves;
Self-blame over losses or illness in your family
Bitterness over failed relationships or unfulfilled dreams
Hurt from negative church experiences
And so much more (you can fill in the blanks here:)
It's time to let go of these "lemons." I say this with love, as someone who's had to let go of many lemons myself.

Practical Steps for Letting Go

Here are some practical steps to help you let go of unforgiveness:

> - Identify what you need to let go of
> - Bring it to the Lord in prayer
> - Visualise yourself releasing it to Jesus
> - Allow Him to renovate that area of your heart

Mark 11:25 (TPT)
"And whenever you stand praying, if you find that you carry something in your heart against another person, release him and forgive him so that your Father in Heaven will also release you and forgive you of your faults."

"If someone believes they are worthless, for whatever reason they tell themselves, then he or she will accept this as truth. They will also make relationships and personal decisions based upon their feeling of worthlessness and beliefs about themselves. On the other hand, if an individual believes they are worthy, then they make choices based upon this belief. What we accept and believe are always correlated to the choices we make in our lives." -Dr Doug Weis Psychologist

Your value is in the fact that God created you and loves you deeply!

Let's take a moment to process what God may have brought up for you.

> *Thank you, Father for revealing to me these things and healing this part of my life. Help me to lean into you and hear your voice throughout my day. I release all my pain, disappointments and broken dreams to you. I ask you to help me forgive…. I choose to forgive them and myself. I choose to forgive You for the things I*

thought You should do. I am sorry I put my expectations on You. Help me to know Your heart. I give You all my lemons. I thank you they turn to dust in Your hands.

REFERENCES:

Family of Origin "FOO" JWFoster
https://www.youtube.com/watch?v=EUzTmaufSgA

"Being With and Shark Music" Circle of Security International
https://www.youtube.com/watch?v=r1ltu26f2cg

Roma Waterman "The Prophetic Plan- 5 day challenge"

Dr Doug Weis Psychologist -the Founder and Executive Director of Heart to Heart Counseling Center

CHAPTER 3
God's character

John 3:16 (NIV)
"For God so loved the world that He gave His one and only Son, that whoever believes in Him shall not perish but have eternal life."

God's Love never quits

This may seem like a strange thing to discuss here. I know many Christians that have been brought up in religious or even Christian families and have ended up with a distorted view of God. This may be because their fathers did not display the image God wanted them to. It may be that your family was very strict and punitive. Maybe your father was not available to you, as he was busy working. This can leave you feeling God is absent, angry, reactive or waiting to punish you. If you view God as this angry punishing God, then you may view parenting life differently. How we view God also changes the way we view ourselves.

What picture of God did you have as a child and now?

It's important to look at how you view God. This will change the way you parent.

So, who is God? This is a hard question to answer, isn't it? Our Heavenly Father gave us His Son, Jesus, and His Word to help us understand who He truly is.

Your "character" is the unique things about you, such as how you act, feel and think. God's character traits are incredibly unique, are never changing and help us understand who He is. We can find these character traits inside the bible God's own Word.

Let's look at what the bible says about Him. Here are a few, there are many more.

God is love: It's the very essence of Him. He sent His Son Jesus who paid the price for our sin by dying on the cross, so we could have a saving relationship with Him. God's love never fails us. It's steady and unconditional. No matter what tomorrow holds or what we may do, nothing can change just how much God loves us.

1 John 4:8 (TPT)
"The one who doesn't love has yet to know God, for God is love."

Romans 8:39 (NLT)
"No power in the sky above or in the earth below — indeed, nothing in all creation will ever be able to separate us from the love of God that is revealed in Christ Jesus our Lord."

God is personal: God has known us personally and intimately since the moment we were conceived. He cares about everything that happens to us. He knows the number of hairs on our head!

Psalm 139:16 (NIV)
"Your eyes saw my unformed body;
all the days ordained for me were written in Your Book
before one of them came to be."

God is Faithful: God has always done what He has said in His Word. This is why our prayers are so powerful when we link them with God's Word. When we have received Jesus as Lord, He will never leave us or forsake us. In fact, He searches for us.

Luke 15:3-7 (NIV)
"Then Jesus told them this parable:
"Suppose one of you has a hundred sheep and loses one of them.
Doesn't he leave the ninety-nine in the open country and
go after the lost sheep until he finds it?
And when he finds it, he joyfully puts it on his shoulders and goes home.

*Then he calls his friends and neighbours together and says,
'Rejoice with me; I have found my lost sheep.'
I tell you that in the same way there will be more rejoicing
in Heaven over one sinner who repents than over ninety-
nine righteous persons who do not need to repent."*

Psalm 94.14 (TPT)
*"For the Lord will never walk away from His cherished ones,
nor would He forsake His chosen ones who belong to Him."*

God is good: God cares deeply for His children

Psalm 37:29 (TPT)
*"The faithful lovers of God will inherit the earth and enjoy
every promise of God's care, dwelling in peace forever."*

James 1:17 (TPT)
*"Every gift God freely gives us is good and perfect,
streaming down from the Father of Lights,
who shines from the heavens with no hidden shadow
or darkness and is never subject to change."*

God is generous: When Jesus was explaining prayer to his disciples, He told them to trust in God's generosity as a sign of his goodness.

Matthew 7:11 (NIV)
"If you, then, though you are evil,

know how to give good gifts to your children,
how much more will your Father in heaven
give good gifts to those who ask him!"

God is Holy: It's hard to think there could be anyone who could be without sin. We have no way of fully understanding God as He is bigger than our minds can conceive. There's no one like God, There's no one who can love like God, provide like God or create like God.

Hebrews 12:29 (TPT)
"For our God is a holy, devouring fire!"

1 Samuel 2:2 (NIV)
"There is no one Holy like the LORD; there is no one besides You; there is no Rock like our God."

2 Corinthians 5:21 (NIV)
"Him who had no sin,"

Isaiah 53:9 (NIV)
"He had done no violence, nor was any deceit in His mouth."

God is merciful: We have done nothing to deserve the gift of being saved from sin. Jesus' sacrifice on the cross opened the door and made the way. There is no greater mercy.

Psalm 116:5
"He was so kind, so gracious to me.

Because of his passion toward me,
he made everything right and he restored me."

God is compassionate: He wants to heal our pain, He is kind and He cares

Psalm 103:8 (TPT)
"Lord, you're so kind and tender-hearted
and so patient with people who fail you!
Your love is like a flooding river overflowing
its banks with kindness."

God is unique: it's hard for us to comprehend.

He is Omnipresent: God is everywhere, always. We are never alone. He is always watching over us.

Psalm 139:7-8 (NIV)
"Where can I go from Your Spirit?
Where can I flee from Your presence?
If I go up to the heavens, You are there;
if I make my bed in the depths, You are there."

He is Omniscient: God knows everything, including everything about us.

Psalm 147:5 (NIV)
"Great is our Lord and mighty in power;
His understanding has no limit."

He is Omnipotent: God has unlimited power. There's absolutely nothing He can't do.

> *Matthew 19:26 (NIV)*
> *"Jesus looked at them and said,*
> *'With man this is impossible,*
> *but with God all things are possible.'"*

There is no greater one, how wonderful that He is willing and able to guide us through motherhood. We are so BLESSED!

Let's pray

> *Heavenly Father please give us a realistic view of who You are so we can show our children Your character through the way we parent. Thank you that You love us unconditionally and are so invested in us and our children.*
>
> *Amen*

I've talked a lot about the nature of God, how much He loves you and how He wants to guide you in your parenting journey. It would be remiss of me not to give you opportunity to ask Jesus to be the Lord of your life. You may have gone to Church regularly, you may know all the things we've talked about in your head, but do you know them in your heart? The gospel is not about following rules, attending church out of obligation or even talking about Jesus. The gospel is about Jesus died for you so you can have relationship with Him. Isn't that absolutely amazing. That relationship comes out of the fact that when Jesus died on the cross, He took all your sins so you could enter into a real relationship with the maker of the world! He is truly wonderful. When God looks at you, He sees Jesus. He will not see any of your sin He will not see any of your flaws, He knows you and loves you as you are. That's why He went to great lengths to bring you into relationship with Him.

Let's pray

> *Jesus. I now know how much You love me and I know You died for my sins so that I could have a relationship with You. I now ask You to come into my life, change me, renew me, guide me and I will promise to seek You always, to sit in Your presence to read Your word to get to know who You are and help me in my life now. I understand now that it's all about being my best friend. Thank you that I can now seek You for anything that's troubling me or just to sit in Your presence and worship You. I am Your child. Help me to find a church that can be family to me in this journey. Amen*

Reckless Love- Song by Bethel Music & Cory Asbury 2020

Before I spoke a word, You were singing over me
You have been so, so good to me
Before I took a breath, You breathed Your life in me
You have been so, so kind to me

Oh, the overwhelming, never-ending, reckless love of God
Oh, it chases me down, fights 'til I'm found, leaves the 99
And I couldn't earn it, and I don't deserve
it, still, You give Yourself away
Oh, the overwhelming, never-ending, reckless love of God

GOD'S CHARACTER

When I was Your foe, still Your love fought for me
You have been so, so good to me
When I felt no worth, You paid it all for me
You have been so, so kind to me

Oh, the overwhelming, never-ending, reckless love of God
Oh, it chases me down, fights 'til I'm found, leaves the 99
And I couldn't earn it, and I don't deserve
it, still, You give Yourself away
Oh, the overwhelming, never-ending, reckless love of God

There's no shadow You won't light up
Mountain You won't climb up
Coming after me
There's no wall You won't kick down
Lie You won't tear down
Coming after me
There's no shadow You won't light up
Mountain You won't climb up
Coming after me
There's no wall You won't kick down
Lie You won't tear down
Coming after me
There's no shadow You won't light up
Mountain You won't climb up
Coming after me
There's no wall You won't kick down
Lie You won't tear down
Coming after me

Oh, the overwhelming, never-ending, reckless love of God
Oh, it chases me down, fights 'til I'm found, leaves the 99

I couldn't earn it, I don't deserve it, still, You give Yourself away
Oh, the overwhelming, never-ending, reckless love of God

Source: Musixmatch Songwriters: Ran Jackson / Cory Asbury / Caleb Culver

CHAPTER 4
Values and Vision

Proverbs 29:18-29 (TPT)
"Where there is no prophetic vision,
people quickly wander astray.
But when you follow the revelation of the Word,
Heaven's bliss fills your soul."

Your Values and Vision

What things are important?

What new traditions do we want to start?

What fun things do we want to be part of family life?

Values are

1. The regard that something is held to deserve; the importance, worth, or usefulness of something. Things that have merit or worth, desirable, significant.

2. Principles or standards of behaviour; one's judgement of what is important in life.

Vision is the ability to think about or plan the future with imagination or wisdom.

This chapter is where you explore what is important to you as a family. How do you want to parent? Take your things you want to carry forward from the last exercise in the earlier chapter and put them on another big piece of paper. Add the other things that are important to you. These might be traditions you want to carry on or just qualities. You can start to put things down like fun, gentleness, honesty, responsiveness, creativity etc. Are there things that come up that you can't agree on? Go back to the Bible and find verses to show you what God would like. Jesus welcomed the little children and rebuked His disciples for trying to keep them away. Ask yourselves: What is important to us as a couple? How can we honour God in our parenting? Attach verses to these values.

Doing this now will help you in making decisions for your child and your life.

Once you have done this you may want to put it up around your home with pictures. Developing values and a vision for your family will also help you to be unified in your parenting. We are often harder on ourselves expecting a certain standard and feel a failure when our child is having a hard time. Remember they are learning how to manage emotions. We don't want to scare them into behaving. We don't want to give them the impression that our love is conditional.

I found these that may be helpful as you work through your values and vision.

> What does the Bible say about parenting?
>
> *Proverbs 22:6.*
> *"Start children off on the way they should go,*
> *and even when they are old they will not turn from it"*
>
> The above verse may be one of the best-known verses concerning parenting. Remarkably, it's just one of more than 1,900 references in the Bible that mention parents, fathers, or mothers. We find most of these references in dozens of stories about complicated families. These stories describe good and bad parenting but contain surprisingly few texts that directly and unambiguously address parent-child dynamics.
>
> It would be great if the Bible contained a parenting script, but it doesn't. While there's no comprehensive passage on parenting, here are 15 key texts concerning the roles, realities, and responsibilities of parents:
>
> **It's recognizing children are a gift and blessing from God.**
>
> *Psalm 127:3*
> *"Children are a heritage from the Lord,*
> *offspring a reward from Him"*

It's helping children love and live for Jesus.

Ephesians 6:4
*"Fathers, do not exasperate your children;
instead, bring them up in the training and instruction of the Lord"*

It's diligently teaching the scriptures to your children.

Deuteronomy 6:6-7
*"These commandments that I give you today are to be on your hearts.
Impress them on your children"*

It's telling your children about the remarkable things God has done.

Psalm 78:4
*"We will tell the next generation the praiseworthy deeds of the Lord,
His power, and the wonders He has done"*

It's inviting children to turn to Jesus, confess their sins, receive the Holy Spirit, and be baptized.

Acts 2:38-39

"Repent and be baptized, every one of you, in the name of Jesus Christ for the forgiveness of your sins. And you will receive the gift of the Holy Spirit. The promise is for you and your children and for all who are far off – for all whom the Lord our God will call"

It's pointing children in the right direction.

Proverbs 22:6
"Start children off on the way they should go,
and even when they are old they will not turn from it"

It's living in a way that makes your children look up to you.

Proverbs 17:6
"Children's children are a crown to the aged,
and parents are the pride of their children"

It's modelling how to live according to a biblical worldview.

Titus 2:7
"In everything set them an example by doing what is good"

It's taking care of your children's needs.

1 Timothy 5:8
"Anyone who does not provide for their relatives,
and especially for their own household,
has denied the faith and is worse than an unbeliever"

It's correcting and disciplining children as a mark of your love.

Proverbs 29:17
"Discipline your children, and they will give you peace;
they will bring you the delights you desire"

It's not irritating, aggravating, disheartening, or provoking children to anger.

Colossians 3:21
"*Fathers, do not embitter your children,
or they will become discouraged*"

It's maintaining harmony and stability in the home.

Proverbs 11:29
"*Whoever brings ruin on their family will inherit only wind,
and the fool will be servant to the wise*"

It's prudent financial planning for your children.

2 Corinthians 12:14
"*Children should not have to save up for their parents,
but parents for their children*"

It's showing your children you respect your own parents.

Deuteronomy 5:16
"*Honour your father and your mother,
as the Lord your God has commanded you*"

> **It's aiming to see your children become mature Christians.**
>
> ### 3 John 1:4
> *"I have no greater joy than to hear that My children are walking in the truth"*
>
> None of this is possible if you're not tracking with Jesus. In the process of parenting, pay attention to your walk with the Lord.
>
> ### Deuteronomy 4:9
> *"Only be careful, and watch yourselves closely so that you do not forget the things your eyes have seen or let them fade from your heart as long as you live. Teach them to your children and to their children after them"*
>
> What does the Bible say about parenting? Taken from https://childrensministrybasics.com/2021/05/11/what-does-the-bible-say-about-parenting/ on 30/4/25

Once you know these you might like to write a mission statement for your family.

If a mission statement doesn't begin to grow organically through Scripture, your life and family values consider simply starting with prayer. Ask God for direction and insight into His plan for your family.

Now you can draw something like this, and write values along the branches:

CHAPTER 5

Practical steps for pregnancy

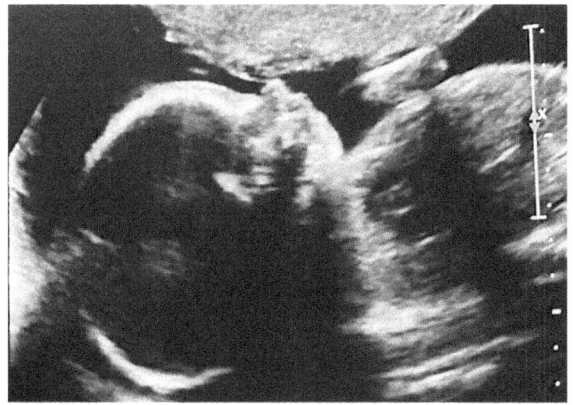

During your pregnancy listen and feel for their likes and dislikes, music, food, your moods. Recent research from the past five years highlights how growing babies can perceive and respond to various maternal stimuli including music, mood, and even dietary choices during pregnancy.

Research continues to back up the amazing design created by God in the process of pregnancy. During pregnancy and after birth, both a mother's brain (matrescence) and a father's brain (patrescence) go through remarkable changes that help prepare them for parenting. Every time you connect with your baby, through touch, cuddles, eye contact, or care, your brain continues to adapt, strengthening your ability to be a responsive and nurturing parent. This transformation enhances what's known as social cognition: the ability to understand your baby's cues, tune in to their emotions, and respond with empathy. When we care for our babies, the brain's reward system is activated, reinforcing that connection and deepening the bond.

Sadly, society often misunderstands or criticizes the deep instincts and choices of mothers. Science shows that these changes are not only real but they're powerful. The simple acts of holding your baby, breathing in their scent, and spending time together shape both your brain and your baby's. It's not just emotional, it's biological.

Brains are always under construction but never as much as in the first 3 years of life. It's quite a journey of intense development with neurons joining up to connect different parts of the brain. This is why we need to be so present and responsive in our care. Even in pregnancy, touch your baby and baby will touch you back. Sing to baby and you will notice his/her reaction. Relaxation strategies for mum will also relax baby.

TALK REGULARLY

You can engage in conversations with your baby during pregnancy. "Chatter boxes" will find this easy but if you are not very verbal you may need to work on this as it is so important. Talk about your day, express your thoughts, or simply speak aloud; your voice provides comfort and stimulation. Talk to your baby every day. We know that research has shown this builds their literacy even in utero. Listen and feel for their response to things.

We now know, fetal hearing begins around 18–20 weeks gestation and 25–27 weeks, babies in utero can respond to sound. By third trimester, they can distinguish between different sounds, including music and voices.

You can even start reading from pregnancy around 20 weeks or earlier. They will love the sound of your voice. Reading books or poems introduces your baby to the rhythm and melody of language, fostering early literacy skills. Prenatal speech exposure develops and strengthens your baby's brain connections. This increased connectivity may support better language development postnatally and potentially influencing language learning later in life.

WHAT IMPACTS CAN MUSIC AND SONG HAVE?

Music and song are so amazing and have many impacts. You can sing to them songs of praise, scripture in song, any song you feel God shows you is for them. Singing lullabies or favourite tunes can soothe your baby and enhance auditory development. This then can help soothe them after they are born as well as the songs will be comforting and familiar. I have a song I have sung to my granddaughter since birth. It's a silly song really but when I started, I did not know the long term impact of me singing it. It is our song. From early on she would stop crying and engage with my face. Now as a 2 year old she laughs with joy when I sing it. Remember, your voice is a powerful tool in nurturing your baby's brain development, even before birth. They don't care how good your voice is! Play a variety of music. Music is amazing it is shown to increase brain capacity. There's a growing body of research suggesting that music exposure during pregnancy and infancy supports neurological, emotional, and social development.

We have seen fetal responses to auditory stimuli. Studies have shown that fetuses can respond to musical stimuli, with observable changes in heart rate patterns: A 2025 study found that playing classical music to unborn babies resulted in more stable and predictable fetal heart rate patterns, suggesting potential developmental benefits for the fetal autonomic nervous system. Another study demonstrated that prenatal exposure to specific musical pieces led to significant increases in fetal heart rate accelerations and movements, indicating a response to music listened to during previous session.

I could detect Kelsie's responses to music when I was pregnant. She loved Sister Act, the movie and she responded with joy when these songs were played after she was born.

Music Reduces Maternal Stress and Anxiety

I find music to be therapeutic to me when I am stressed. I will put on worship music to remind me that God is in control, and I am in His hands. I then can work on reducing stress and choose to take the peaceful road. We now know that research indicates that maternal stress and anxiety during pregnancy can affect fetal behaviour and development. For instance, elevated maternal stress levels have been associated with changes in fetal heart rate and movement patterns. When a pregnant person listens to calming music, it helps lower cortisol levels (the stress hormone). So if we know that lower maternal stress leads to healthier fetal development this is something we can use to benefit both you and your baby. Studies have shown that listening to music for 30 minutes daily significantly reduced maternal anxiety and depression, with positive implications for the fetus. We also know that singing and humming stimulates the vagus nerve which leads to better health for you. Worship is good for our relationship with God and our health. Singing improves emotional, spiritual, psychological, behavioural and physiological health. Worship is something we can do to bless God as well.

Music Supports Brain Development

Exposure to music enhances areas of the brain responsible for language, emotion, and motor coordination. Infants who engaged in interactive music sessions (e.g., clapping, moving with rhythm) showed stronger brain responses to musical and speech sounds.

Music Strengthens Bonding

Singing lullabies and playing music helps strengthen the emotional bond between caregivers and babies. It also helps regulate babies' emotions and encourages social interaction. Responsive musical interactions like singing during diaper changes or soothing with lullabies have been shown to increase secure attachment behaviours.

DIET

If you can, try to eat the rainbow of foods each day, exercise regularly and rest as much as you are able when you are tired. It is good to consider dietary choices: A varied and balanced diet not only supports maternal health but may also influence your baby's future food preferences. Isn't that amazing! While specific studies from the past five years are limited, earlier research has shown that flavours from the maternal diet can pass into the amniotic fluid, exposing the fetus to various tastes. This prenatal exposure may influence postnatal food preferences.

This following article from Healthline reports Research suggests mental health and the gut are linked through the gut-brain axis.

Here's how to take care of your gut:

> Anxiety can feel overwhelming, bringing on everything from racing thoughts and restlessness to full-blown panic attacks. While therapy, lifestyle changes, and sometimes medication are key parts of managing anxiety, one often-overlooked piece of the puzzle is gut health.
>
> There's growing evidence that the balance of bacteria and other microorganisms in the gut—known as the gut microbiota—is closely linked to mental health, particularly conditions like anxiety and depression.
>
> For instance, research has shown that individuals with anxiety often experience reduced microbial diversity and imbalances in gut bacteria.
>
> When the gut is out of balance, it can contribute to inflammation and the production of mood-regulating neurotransmitters like serotonin. Supporting gut health may help reduce anxiety symptoms and improve overall mental well-being.

Here are a few evidence-informed ways to improve gut health that may also help support emotional balance:-

Choose whole, gut-friendly foods

Knowing which foods contribute to a healthy gut and which may cause problems is a great place to start.

Diet plays a major role in the health of the gut microbiome. Highly processed foods, added sugars, and saturated fat can feed harmful bacteria and promote inflammation, two factors that may negatively impact mental health.

Try replacing ultra-processed, high-sugar, and high fat foods with whole foods. These foods include:

High fiber foods: Broccoli, Brussels sprouts, oats, peas, avocados, pears, bananas, and berries are full of fiber, which aids in healthy digestion.

Foods high in omega-3 fatty acids: Salmon, mackerel, walnuts, chia seeds, and flaxseed are packed with omega-3s, which may help reduce inflammation and improve digestion.

Eat probiotics and prebiotic-rich foods

A balanced gut microbiome relies on both probiotics (beneficial bacteria) and prebiotics (the fibers that feed them). Including a mix of both can help support microbial diversity, which is linked to better mental and digestive health.

> Ways to incorporate probiotics and prebiotics into your diet include:
>
> Some Probiotic foods are sauerkraut, kefir, kimchi, kombucha, apple cider vinegar, kvass, high quality yogurt
>
> Some Prebiotic-rich foods are jicama, asparagus, chicory root, dandelion greens, onions, garlic and leeks

PRAY

What an awesome opportunity. It's so much better when the heavy load can be shouldered by Jesus. You get to set aside time to pray for them each day. It's helpful if you can find scriptures to pray over them. Maybe choose a few for each day of the week or one a day for each month.

Here are a few as you find more just add to these!

PROTECTION AND SAFETY

Psalm 91:11
"For He will command His angels concerning you to guard you in all your ways."

Prayer: Lord, command Your angels to guard this little one in all their ways. Keep them safe wherever they go.

Isaiah 54:17
"No weapon formed against you shall prosper..."

Prayer: I declare that no weapon formed against this little one will prosper. Protect their body, mind, and spirit.

FAITH AND SALVATION

Isaiah 54:13
"All your children shall be taught by the Lord, and great shall be the peace of your children."

Prayer: Lord, teach this little one Your truth. Let their heart be filled with Your peace.

2 Timothy 3:15
"...from childhood you have known the Holy Scriptures, which are able to make you wise for salvation through faith in Christ Jesus."

Prayer: May this little one grow up knowing Your Word and finding salvation in Jesus.

Matthew 22:37
"He said to him, you shall love the Lord God with all your heart, with all your soul, and with all your mind."

Prayer: "Lord, I pray that my little one would know You and they would experience Your love. That he/she would know Your presence, his/her entire heart and soul, and mind would be filled with the presence of God. That he/she may intimately experience <u>a relationship</u> with You.

WISDOM AND GUIDANCE

Proverbs 3:5–6
"Trust in the Lord with all your heart...
He will make your paths straight."

Prayer: Teach this little one to trust in You. Guide his/her steps and direct his/her path.

James 1:5
"If any of you lacks wisdom,
let him ask of God..."

Prayer: Give this little one wisdom for every decision, and a heart that seeks You first.

Psalm 32:8
"I will instruct you and teach you in the way which you should
I will counsel you with my eye upon you."

Prayer: "Lord, I pray that You would instruct my little one and teach him/her in the way that he/she should go, that You will counsel him/her with Your eye upon him/her."

Proverbs 16:3,9
"Commit your works to the Lord and your plans will be established...
The mind of man plans his way but the Lord directs his steps."

Prayer: *"Father, I pray that my little one will commit his/her works and plans to the Lord. That You would establish his/her steps and show him/her exactly the way to go.*

Ephesians 6:14-15 (NKJV)
Stand therefore, having girded your waist with truth,
having put on the breastplate of righteousness,
and having shod your feet with the
preparation of the gospel of peace;

Prayer: *"I pray that my child will learn early how to put on the armour You have provided"*

PEACE AND CONFIDENCE

Philippians 4:6–7 (NKJV)
Be anxious for nothing,
but in everything by prayer and supplication, with thanksgiving,
let your requests be made known to God;
and the peace of God, which surpasses all understanding,
will guard your hearts and minds through Christ Jesus.

Prayer: *Calm this little ones' heart and mind. Let Your peace rule over any fear or anxiety.*

2 Timothy 1:7
"For God has not given us a spirit of fear,
but of power and of love and of a sound mind."

Prayer: *Fill this little one with courage, love, and a sound mind today and always.*

IDENTITY AND PURPOSE

Jeremiah 29:11
For I know the thoughts that I think toward you, says the Lord, thoughts of peace and not of evil, to give you a future and a hope.

Prayer: *Thank You for the good plans You have for this little one. Help him/her walk boldly in Your purpose.*

Psalm 139:14
"I praise You because I am fearfully and wonderfully made…"

Prayer: May this little one know his/her worth and identity in You. Let him/her never doubt he/she is wonderfully made.

Philippians 1:6
"For I am confident of this very thing,
that He who began a good work in you
will perfect it until the day of Christ Jesus."

Prayer: *"I pray that you will begin the good work in my little one and continue to perfect it and refine it and further it in his/her heart and he/she will live out the good work that You have planned for him/her."*

1 Corinthians 10:13
"No temptation has overtaken you that is not common to man.
God is faithful, He will not let you be tempted beyond your ability.
But with the temptation,
He will also provide the way of escape
that you will be able to endure."

Prayer: "Lord, I pray over my child that no temptation will overtake him/her, because You are faithful, You will not let them be tempted beyond his/her ability, but You will provide a way of escape. I declare this over his/her life and over his/her choices and over his/her future in Jesus name!"

BLESSING AND FAVOR

Numbers 6:24–26
"The Lord bless you and keep you;
the Lord make His face shine upon you…"

Prayer: Lord, bless and keep this little one. Make Your face shine on him/her and give him/her peace.

Psalm 5:12
"Surely, Lord, You bless the righteous;
You surround them with Your favour as with a shield."

Prayer: Surround this little one with Your favour like a shield in every area of his/her life.

Use these bible verses to pray over your kids daily

We are equipped to protect our children with the help of the Lord. I am believing for our children that they are born for such a time as this and God will help them rise up to an incredible purpose that God has prepared. They are going to shift and change this world in ways we can't even imagine. All we have to do lean on Him and be their prayer warriors. Focus on these Bible verses to pray to help your kids become the world changers God has called them to be!

<u>In summary- We can start to connect with our baby before birth.</u>

Engage with your baby: Talking, singing, praying and playing music can help fetal development and foster early bonding.

In Pregnancy:

- Listen to a variety of soft, melodic music (classical, lullabies, or nature sounds).
- Sing to your baby, your voice is especially comforting.
- Pray from now every day for protection and guidance for our babies.

After Birth:

- Play gentle music during routines (bathing, bedtime).
- Encourage musical play: rattles, baby drums, clapping.
- Sing regularly, even if off-key, your baby will love it.
- Continue to pray each day

Maintain emotional well-being: Managing stress and promoting positive emotions can have beneficial effects on both maternal and fetal health. If you are struggling with mental health issues please see someone now to get some help before the baby arrives.

REFERENCES:

Nurture Revolution – 2024 by Greer Kirshenbaum PhD (Author)

Partanen et al. (2013) found that fetuses exposed to a specific lullaby in the womb showed brain responses to that same melody four months after birth, demonstrating prenatal memory and auditory learning.

Prenatal experience with language shapes the brain. https://www.science.org/doi/10.1126/sciadv.adj3524 Down loaded 26/5/25

https://www.sciencetimes.com/articles/47290/20231124/unborn-babies-exposed-language-womb-influence-later-learning-study-suggests.htm Downloaded 26/5/25

https://www.frontiersin.org/journals/human-neuroscience/articles/10.3389/fnhum.2024.1379660/full Downloaded 26/5/25

Prenatal influences on postnatal neuroplasticity: Integrating DOHaD and sensitive/critical period frameworks to understand biological embedding in early development. https://pmc.ncbi.nlm.nih.gov/articles/PMC11647198/ Downloaded 26/5/25

Response to music on the nonlinear dynamics of human fetal heart rate fluctuations: A recurrence plot analysis. https://pubmed.ncbi.nlm.nih.gov/39903054/ Downloaded 2025

Partanen, E., Kujala, T., Huotilainen, M., et al. (2013). Learning-induced neural plasticity of speech processing before birth. *Proceedings of the National Academy of Science*s, 110(37), 15145–15150. https://doi.org/10.1073/pnas.1302159110

Effects of prenatal stress on pregnancy and human development: mechanisms and pathways https://pmc.ncbi.nlm.nih.gov/articles/PMC9995932/

https://pubmed.ncbi.nlm.nih.gov/38866136/

Chang, M. Y., Chen, C. H., & Huang, K. F. (2008). Effects of music therapy on psychological health of women during pregnancy. *Journal of Clinical Nursing*, 17(19), 2580–

https://www.singupfoundation.org/about-singing-for-mental-health/understanding-singing-for-mental-health/singing-health#:~:text=A%20key%20part%20of%20the,Singing%20helps%20with%20pain.

Zhao, T. C., & Kuhl, P. K. (2016). Musical intervention enhances infants' neural processing of temporal structure in music and speech. *Proceedings of the National Academy of Sciences*, 113(19), 5212–5217.

https://doi.org/10.1073/pnas.1603984113

Trehub, S. E., & Trainor, L. J. (1998). Singing to infants: Lullabies and play songs. *Advances in Infancy Research*, 12, 43–77.

HEALTHLINE RESOURCE https://www.healthline.com/health/digestive-health/mental-health-gut-health Downloaded 8/6/25

Downloaded and modified From https://stefaniegass.com/blog/bible-verses-to-pray/ 21/5/25

CHAPTER 6

Establishing a support network – Finding your Village.

Matthew 18:20
For where two or three gather together in My name, there am I with them."

WHO HOLDS WHO

- Mother holds the baby
- Father holds the mother
- Family holds the new family
- Community holds all
- Who holds you in this time?

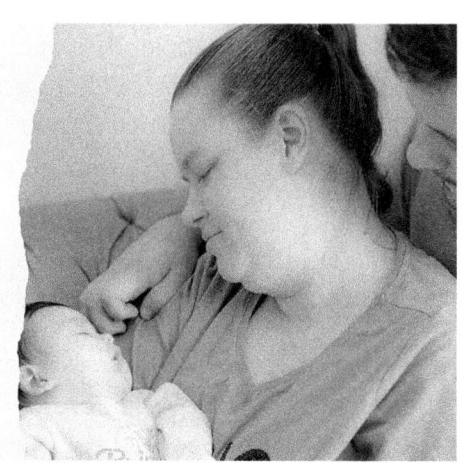

WHAT IS A VILLAGE?

It's your group of people you trust and who share similar ideas about parenting. They're the ones you turn to for support, encouragement, and advice. Your village might include family members, friends from church, neighbours, or others in your community. You'll need more than just one person, because no one can do it all.

Not everyone in your support network will agree with you on everything and that's okay.

You might have:

- Someone you can call anytime, or someone who'll drop everything to come help.
- A friend who brings meals or helps you get the house back in order.
- A listener, the one who checks in when you're feeling low.
- The no-nonsense friend who tells it like it is, with love.
- The breastfeeding friend to help you understand how it works.

Make a list of these people. Then grab a calendar and work out who might be available on different days after your baby arrives. Having this in place ahead of time helps take the pressure off when you need support.

WHAT IF YOU DON'T HAVE A VILLAGE YET?

There's still time to build one. Look around, are there neighbours who always say hello? Maybe ask them for coffee and see where it leads. Consider joining a church; it can provide not just support for you and your partner, but lasting friendships for your child too.

ESTABLISHING A SUPPORT NETWORK- FINDING YOUR VILLAGE.

Start nurturing those relationships now. Pay attention to the people who are generous, calm, helpful, or good listeners. Let them into your world a little during your pregnancy so they're already close when the baby comes. Find a trusted source of information and support, real people, not just Google or AI.

THINGS WILL SHIFT AFTER BABY ARRIVES.

The friends you chatted with at work won't be as available when you're on maternity leave, and you might not be as free to chat either. They may be at a different life stage to you. That's why connecting with other mums is so important.

FRIENDSHIPS MAY CHANGE

- Different priorities
- Different conversations
- More difficult to go places
- Focus on baby things
- Less available cash
- Tired

If you can, join a mums' group before your baby arrives, it'll be easier to show up when the time comes. I know it's a bit nerve wracking turning up that first time. It gets easier after that. These groups can be wonderful, but finding your village takes time. New parent groups often only run for a few weeks, and not every group will feel like a good fit for you. Try to find mums who live nearby so you can catch up more easily. Being with others in the same season of life makes a big difference.

Just remember, everyone parents differently. Some friendships may shift if your views don't align and that's okay. You get to decide what's right for you and your baby.

The internet can offer quick answers, but it doesn't know your baby. It can also lead you down overwhelming rabbit holes and stir up unnecessary anxiety. Stick to a few trusted sites for helpful info.

THIS JOURNEY MIGHT NOT LOOK ANYTHING LIKE YOU IMAGINED.

Social media and TV paint an unrealistic picture of what babies "should" do. Let go of those expectations, most of them are myths. And remember, even other mums' memories can be fuzzy or rose-tinted. Trust yourself and your instincts as you find your way. Your baby will be unique, and others may not understand them. That's ok because only you need to at this stage.

WEIGHING UP HOW TO NAVIGATE IN-LAWS

Not all in-laws are difficult, but they do come with different experiences, traditions, and expectations. Because of this, their input might sometimes feel uncomfortable, even if it's well-meaning.

Understanding where your in-laws are coming from can be helpful. Exploring your partner's family dynamics, what it was like for him growing up, how his parents handled challenges, and what roles were expected, can offer insight into why they may behave or believe the way they do. Hopefully, you and your partner have already reflected on your own family of origin and discussed your shared values and vision for your new family. That foundation is key.

Parenting styles are deeply influenced by generational norms. What felt "normal" to your in-laws when raising children might now feel outdated or misaligned with your approach. It can be particularly tricky when unsolicited advice or subtle criticism begins to chip away at your confidence. In these moments, it's important to remind yourself: you are the parent now.

SO HOW DO YOU NAVIGATE THIS WELL?

Start with your partner. He likely understands both his family and your needs better than anyone. Talk openly and respectfully about how you're feeling. Let him take the lead when it comes to setting boundaries with his own family. This often works best and avoids placing you in the position of "the bad guy."

A **unified front** is essential. It tells others that you're a team and helps avoid confusion or triangulation (when others try to play one of you against the other). Decide together what your boundaries are and agree on how you'll communicate them. Whether it's about visits, holding the baby, feeding choices, or parenting practices, being clear and kind is powerful.

Sometimes, it helps to give your in-laws ways to feel involved that align with your values. Maybe they'd love to cook a meal or help with laundry, rather than offering constant opinions about sleep routines or feeding. Finding safe, helpful ways for them to contribute can help keep the relationship positive.

But also know this: **you're allowed to set limits.** You don't have to accept every opinion, suggestion, or expectation. Respect can still exist within firm boundaries.

Over time, your in-laws may come to see and respect your parenting choices, especially when they see your child thriving in your care. Until then, lean on your partner, stay grounded in your values, and give yourself permission to protect your peace.

HANDLING UNWANTED ADVICE

Unwanted advice often comes from a place of care and concern, but that doesn't make it any less frustrating. Navigating it gracefully takes a little patience, some strategy, and a lot of confidence in yourself. Here are some gentle ways to handle it:

Listen First

Sometimes advice is worth hearing. Simply listening without reacting can ease defensiveness and help you decide whether there's anything useful in what's being shared.

Smile and Disregard

If the advice doesn't align with your values, you can always smile, nod, and respond with something neutral like, *"That's interesting!"*, then carry on with your own approach.

Agree Where You Can

Acknowledging the helpful or well-intentioned parts of someone's comment can keep the peace, even if you don't plan to follow their advice.

Pick Your Battles

Not every issue is worth the emotional energy. You might let small things slide (like whether the baby wears a hat) but stand firm on the things that really matter to you.

Avoid Trigger Topics

If you know certain topics will invite opinions you don't want, it's okay to steer clear of them in conversation.

Know Your Stuff

The more informed you are, the more confident you'll feel. Knowledge is empowering and can help you brush off unwanted advice with ease.

Share Gently

If someone's advice is clearly outdated or inaccurate, gently offer more current information. A respectful approach can sometimes shift their perspective.

Quote the Experts

Backing up your decisions with expert guidance, like your midwife, GP, or a trusted parenting book, can lend credibility and take the pressure off you personally. You can always say the midwife or child nurse said this is new research.

Be Vague When Needed

Not every conversation needs a detailed explanation. Say something like, *"We're working through that,"* or *"We've got a plan,"* and leave it there.

Ask for Advice Strategically

If someone is eager to help, ask them for input on something neutral (like freezer meal tips). This can satisfy their desire to be involved without touching on your parenting values.

Have a Standard Reply Ready

Something like, *"That might not be right for everyone, but it's working well for us,"* can help you gracefully shut down repeated advice.

Speak Honestly

If advice becomes overwhelming, it's okay to calmly express your preferences and ask for space to parent your way.

Bring in a Mediator

If the tension builds, a trusted mutual friend or family member may help bridge the gap.

Find Your People

Surround yourself with those who share your parenting style or values. Support from like-minded friends can make a big difference.

Above all, remember this is *your* baby, and *your* choices matter most. Trust yourself, you're the one who knows your child best.

Navigating Changing Roles for You and Your Partner

Talk with your partner before the baby arrives about how life will shift.

You'll need support with the baby, the house, meals, laundry, and everything in between. Don't expect to keep up with everything you do now. Even though you won't be heading off to a job, you'll be working harder than ever before. This is your first 24/7 role and it's intense.

Start sharing the load early.

If you have pets, for example, now's the time to pass their care to your partner. Pets who were once the centre of attention can feel displaced when a baby arrives. If they sleep in your bedroom, consider gradually moving them to a different space before the baby is born, to ease the transition.

Meals can be simplified or delegated.

Perhaps your partner takes over the cooking for a while, or you line up a meal delivery service for the early weeks. Either way, make a plan now so you're not trying to figure it out in the thick of newborn life.

Laundry will multiply overnight.

Babies go through clothes quickly and so will you. Make sure your partner is familiar with how the washing machine works and feels confident doing laundry. It's an easy skill to learn now, and it makes a big difference later.

When a baby is born, parents are born too.

Now there are three people in your home and one of them will need far more help than the others: *you*. You'll be recovering physically and navigating huge emotional changes. Your baby will need you constantly. It's deeply rewarding and completely exhausting.

Plan to stay close in those early weeks.

If possible, be home together as you settle in. Let everything slow down. This time is about learning your new rhythm and discovering life as a family. In the fog of sleep deprivation and newness, staying connected and present makes all the difference.

CHAPTER 7

Breastfeeding

E mpowering mothers, nourishing babies.

PSALM 22:9-10 (NKJV)
"But You are He who took me out of the womb;
You made me trust while on my mother's breasts.
I was cast upon You from birth.
From my mother's womb You have been My God."

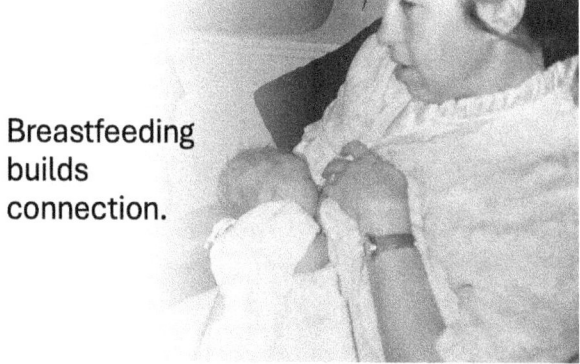

Breastfeeding builds connection.

Breastfeeding is the way God has designed us to feed and comfort our babies. It's a process of surrender to your new role in nurturing your baby as a mother. In life you have many competing jobs, in pregnancy your brain changes to tell you to shut out a lot of those things you used to do, so it can focus on your baby. In our society we have these expectations of babies that are unrealistic. Society expects babies to feed and then not bother us for a while as they sleep. Breastfeeding is relationship, it's not just food, so the trust relationship is built by responding to baby's needs. Try not to go down the rabbit hole of weighing up if they've had enough food last feed and why are they hungry now. Baby cries, and comes to the breast to be settled, the breast is you, in relationship you bring the baby to you. The baby has a need, you respond by offering the breast. At the breast baby suckles and is calmed, and in the process gains nutrition.

Breastmilk is complex and offers baby so much, it develops their immune system, it fights infection, it protects against disease both for you and baby.

Breastmilk provides hormones to help them sleep and grow. On a gut level each time you feed you are feeding baby's gut, so you see it's not a three, or four hour thing but is built on intermittent responsive care. We often want our baby not to disturb the other things we need to do, instead of realising that nurturing our baby is the thing we need to do.

We celebrate the gift of breastfeeding and its profound impact on health, connection and happiness.

> **To Be a Mother- Intimacy- into me I see.**
>
> *My heart is full*
> *I look at you and my love is deep.*
> *You are a little bit of heaven on earth.*
> *I look at you changing before my eyes, growing into the person you are.*
> *The amazing creative loving child*
> *I am tired*
> *But you my dear baby I would not trade you for all the money in the world*
> *You watch me and copy me.*
> *You cling to me though I am not perfect.*
> *You helped me find myself, not the one I portray to the world*
> *But the one deep inside.*
> *Thank you precious one.*
> *Thank you for finding me.*
>
> *Written by Jenni Helm*

GENERATIONAL BELIEFS ABOUT BREASTFEEDING

Family attitudes toward breastfeeding can deeply impact a mother's feeding choices. If you were raised in a family where breastfeeding was encouraged and normalized, you might feel more supported in your journey. However, if breastfeeding was discouraged, viewed as inconvenient, or surrounded by myths, you might experience uncertainty, even if you want to breastfeed. It's important to recognize these generational influences and seek evidence-based information and support to make informed feeding decisions. You have the power to break cycles of misinformation and reclaim confidence in your body's ability to nourish your baby.

Proverbs 5:19 (TPT)
Let her breasts be your satisfaction, and let her embrace intoxicate you at all times. Be continually delighted and ravished with her love!

God has given us the ability to nourish our babies with all they need. Breastmilk changes with your baby's needs as they grow. Breastmilk is the natural and normal way to feed babies, and it's packed with amazing benefits that go way beyond just keeping them full.

Breastfeeding is a beautiful journey, but preparation is key!

Here's how to get ready:

1. Understand how breastfeeding works. A little knowledge goes a long way!

2. Build your village. Surround yourself with supportive people—your partner, family, and friends who've breastfed successfully.

3. Plan an antenatal lactation visit, especially if it is all new to you. Chat with a lactation consultant before your baby arrives.

4. Line up early lactation support if needed. Have resources ready for those first precious days. If things feel hard seek help early.

> *Psalms 131:2 (TPT)*
> *"I am humbled and quieted in your presence.*
> *Like a contented child who rests on it's mother's lap,*
> *I'm Your resting child and my soul is content in You."*

Breastmilk: More Than Just Food -Designed by God **for Baby**

Why is breastfeeding so good? We are still learning everyday about this. Did you know, when your baby starts to get sick, the breastfeeding mother's immune system picks this up by a backwash system and develops antibodies quickly to fight illness?

What's in Breastmilk? The nutritional components of breastmilk are made in the milk making cells of the breast. They are sourced from the mother's diet or from maternal stores.

Breastfeeding helps with immune health: Breastmilk is all goodness and it's linked strongly with gut health. The gut microbiome is a complex community of bacteria, viruses, fungi, and other microorganisms that live in the digestive tract. For babies, this microbiome plays a crucial role in digestion, immune system development, and overall health. Breastfeeding has a huge impact on shaping a baby's gut microbiome in several ways.

Breastfeeding reduces the risk of infections and inflammatory conditions by **promoting beneficial bacteria** and preventing harmful bacteria from taking over. It helps **train the immune system** by introducing antibodies, immune cells, and anti-inflammatory compounds. This is especially so in the first few days. Colostrum starts the process to trigger immune system.

Breast Milk as a Prebiotic and Probiotic: Breast milk contains **human milk oligosaccharides (HMOs).** These are special sugars that feed beneficial bacteria, particularly *Bifidobacteria*, which support gut and immune function (prebiotics). Breast milk also contains **live bacteria**, acting as a probiotic to promote a diverse and healthy microbiome (probiotics). **Differences Between Breastfed and Formula-Fed Babies' Microbiomes:** Breastfed babies tend to have a gut microbiome dominated by **Bifidobacteria and Lactobacilli,** which protect against infections and inflammation. Formula-fed babies typically have a more diverse but less beneficial microbiome, often containing more potentially pathogenic bacteria. What are the **long-term health benefits?** A well-balanced microbiome lowers the risk of allergies, asthma, obesity, and autoimmune diseases. Studies suggest breastfeeding is linked to a lower risk of digestive disorders like colic, constipation, and even long-term conditions like inflammatory bowel disease (IBD). **Breastfeeding exclusively for at least 6 months** and beyond can maximize microbiome benefits. Vaginal birth and **skin-to-skin contact** can also help transfer beneficial bacteria.

Proteins- The most abundant proteins in breastmilk are casein, α-lactalbumin, lactoferrin, secretory immunoglobulin IgA, lysozyme and serum albumin. These proteins help fight germs and support baby's growth and development.

Fats – Fats are important to provide energy, keep baby satisfied and are vital brain-building nutrients. Fat is variable and changes with maternal diet. It changes during the feed, being lower at the beginning of feed and higher as feed progresses. An empty breast means higher fat component. It's important to know a mother that consumes more long chain polyunsaturated fatty acids (eg omega-3 fatty acids in her diet), will produce breastmilk that will contain higher proportions of those fats.

Breastmilk contains various growth factors which have significant effects on the developing baby's gut, blood vessels, nervous system and endocrine system. **Hormones and growth factors** help develop their organs and systems.

Carbohydrates (lactose) give baby energy and special sugars called **oligosaccharides help develop good gut bacteria by feeding them. Good gut bacteria protect baby from illness and harmful bacteria. White blood cells** and even **stem cells are present.** Research is still investigating impacts of these.

Vitamins and Minerals are generally sourced from food, but a few mums might need extra: **B12** if you're vegan or vegetarian. **Vitamin D** if you are low in Vitamin D your baby will be. **Iodine**, which is recommended during pregnancy and breastfeeding.

IN SUMMARY

Breastmilk: A Dynamic and Protective Fluid designed by God to nurture your baby.

Biological Norm: Breastfeeding is the natural way to feed human babies, and breastmilk is uniquely designed to meet their needs.

Immune and Developmental Support: It contains protective and developmental components that support a baby's **immune system, gut health**, and **overall growth**.

Changes Over Time: Breastmilk evolves throughout your breastfeeding journey, during each feed, and changes to meet babies needs as they grow older. Breastmilk differs between mothers, and between preterm and term babies.

Breastmilk is an evolving, complex fluid uniquely tailored by God to nourish, protect, and help your baby thrive. Its full range of benefits goes far beyond basic nutrition, and many of its components are still being discovered by science.

GOOD FOR MUM

Breastfeeding doesn't just benefit babies; it also offers powerful health benefits for **mothers**. Breastfeeding is good for your **body**, your **mind**, and your **future health**. It's not just a gift to your baby it is designed to protect and nurture you, too.

Here's how breastfeeding protects and supports mums:

1. **Helps Your Body Recover After Birth**

   Breastfeeding triggers the release of **oxytocin**, a hormone that helps your uterus contract and return to its pre-pregnancy size more quickly. This same hormone also helps reduce postpartum blood loss.

2. **Supports Emotional Wellbeing**

   The hormones released during breastfeeding (like **oxytocin and prolactin**) can promote **relaxation, bonding**, and a sense of **calm** which can help reduce stress and lower the risk of **postnatal depression**. These have limited effects when mums are stressed by pressures internally or externally and they may need to work at relaxation techniques to allow impacts. It is a common myth that breastfeeding is more stressful on mental health. If breastfeeding is hard, support from knowledgeable people can go a long way to be able to resolve this.

3. **Natural Birth Spacing**

   Breastfeeding (especially exclusive breastfeeding) can in some people **delay the return of ovulation** and periods in the early months, which may help space pregnancies naturally. This is known as the **lactational amenorrhea method (LAM).** It's important to use additional birth protection if it is crucial another baby is not appropriate or wanted at this time.

4. **Lowers Risk of Certain Diseases**

   Breastfeeding is linked to a lower risk of several health conditions later in life such as **Breast cancer, Ovarian cancer, Type 2 diabetes, High blood pressure,** and **Heart disease**. The longer you breastfeed, the stronger these protective effects seem to be.

5. **Supports Healthy Weight**

   Breastfeeding burns extra calories, around **500 per day** which can help support postpartum weight loss (though this varies between women).

6. **Builds Confidence and Connection.**

   Breastfeeding can boost confidence as you learn to understand and respond to your baby's needs. Many mothers feel a **deep sense of connection** and empowerment through the breastfeeding journey.

BEGINNING YOUR BREASTFEEDING JOURNEY

The First Milk – Colostrum

The first fluid, made by breastfeeding mothers is called colostrum. It is golden in colour and is all goodness, despite being made in small amounts it is a rich source of immune protective factors (e.g. secretory IgA, lactoferrin, white blood cells) and developmental factors (e.g. epidermal growth factor). Designed to line your baby's gut and set their immune response for life. It is full of **immune-boosting goodies** like antibodies and white blood cells. Colostrum is produced during pregnancy and at birth. This boosts **initial colonization of your baby at birth.** A baby's microbiome is now believed to start in pregnancy and then changes during birth. Vaginal birth exposes the baby to beneficial maternal bacteria, primarily *Lactobacillus* species, which help establish a healthy gut. Skin to skin immediately after birth can also help baby to pick up healthy bacteria. We know C-section babies may have delayed colonization and a different microbial composition, but breastfeeding can help balance this.

Ask for baby to be placed uninterrupted on your belly for the first few of hours. Baby will be very alert in this time looking up in amazement at you and your partner. Then their instincts will start to kick in and they can search for and find the breast on their own or with sometimes a little help from you. Remember to talk them through this process. Your voice is like their anchor. They may feed for a little or for a long time. They then will settle to sleep right there. Baby does not need volume as they are born waterlogged especially if you have had an IV drip during the birth process. Babies put down fat stores on their body in the last few weeks of pregnancy to draw on till milk comes in. Colostrum is all they need for the first few days.

Feeding will be often and irregular, timing is when they look hungry licking their lips and turning their head or looking at you. Crying is a later sign and it's good to feed before they get to this stage. Length of feeds can be from a few minutes to up to 45 mins. Offer both sides each feed but it doesn't matter if they don't take the second side.

Awake time will be short and sweet initially. Babies are often only awake for feeds and nappy change then off to sleep again. Take any opportunity to talk to and cuddle your baby. You can't spoil them. You don't have to put them down if you don't want to.

Babies feed often in first few days, offer them the breast each time they stir. Day 2 baby will most likely feed, feed, feed. This will help bring your milk in. Around day 3 after birth, a mother's breastmilk 'comes in' and this increases milk production to support the needs of your rapidly growing baby.

For the first 5-6 weeks your milk supply comes from hormonal influences and removal of milk from your breast from baby suckling and from expressing if needed. After that extraction of milk is the only thing that keeps your supply up.

Breastfeeding should not hurt! When baby latches deeply they will have an open mouth and there will be no clicking or loosing the breast. It may feel weird or sensitive but if there is pain gently take baby off by inserting your finger in the side of mouth to break the suction and try again. Baby comes to the breast as you would if you were eating a hamburger lower lip first then reaching up and just over the nipple. This allows the nipple to be drawn deeper into baby's mouth as they suck. Drawing the nipple deep, so it is not compressed on the hard pallet, enables the baby to suck without any pain to you.

How will you know baby is getting enough? Watch their nappies and they usually will fill out, cheeks and arms and legs as well as having a bigger tummy after the feed.

What to expect in nappies.

We expect baby will do: Day 1- 1 poo and 1 wee (24 hrs), Day 2- 2 poos and 2 wees, Day 3- 3 poos and 3 wees, Day 4- 4 poos and 4 wees, Day 5- 5 poos and 5 wees. From then on, we expect baby will have 5-6 wet nappies and multiple poos each day. Baby's gut initially will be quite quick as it adjusts to feeding and digesting food. Then is settles a bit and poos become less often but still soft, mustard in color and quite a few.

Baby's weight

Babies loose up to 10% of their body weight in the first week. Some of this is excess fluid from birth. We expect they will gain back that weight by 2 weeks. Most babies will then gain 150-200gms per week. You will notice that they are growing and putting on fat. Their clothes will show you as they grow and fill them then need to go up to the next size. Babies may put on a little one week then a lot the next week, growth is not linear.

The big picture

If you are worried about your baby look at the big picture. Are they bright and vigorous when awake? Are they seeking the breast and feeding well? Do they have enough wet and dirty nappies? You very quickly will know what their normal looks like. If you are still worried trust your instincts and get baby checked.

> *Genesis 49:25 (TPT)*
> *"The God of your father will help and protect you; the God who is more than enough will bless you. He will bless you with the blessings of Heaven, blessings of the deep that lie beneath, and blessings of the breast and womb."*

As you can see breastmilk is amazing stuff created by our maker God for us specifically for your baby. If you are having pain or other issues reach out for help early from an International Breastfeeding Certified Lactation Consultant (IBCLC).

This book is not designed to give you all the information on breastfeeding but more an introduction.

What happens when things don't feel right, or breastfeeding does not seem to work well? Sometimes when people have needed help to conceive and maintain pregnancy, their hormones may be out of balance. This in turn can impact breastfeeding. It is vital to get support from an IBCLC. If this is your story it may help to seek out support earlier even before birth. If you cannot supply your baby with all the food they need, It does not need to be either breastfeeding or formula. Any breastmilk is good for your baby.

Breastfeeding grief is real and is the deep emotional sadness, guilt, or sense of loss a mother may feel when breastfeeding doesn't go as planned whether it ends earlier than hoped, doesn't happen at all, or doesn't meet her expectations.

Grief can catch many mothers off guard, especially when she knows how breast is the biological normal way to feed her baby designed by God. Women need support to give them the best chance of success and honour the complexity of their journeys.

Common reasons for struggling with breastfeeding/grief:

Struggling to breastfeed despite trying everything.
Pressure to formula feed from your main supports.
Low milk supply or baby not gaining enough weight
Needing to compliment breastfeeds with formula from lack of supply.
Pain or physical trauma (e.g. cracked nipples, mastitis)
Returning to work or external pressures
Lack of support or conflicting advice
Medical complications (baby's or mother's) that may have led to traumatic birth

What does it feel like?

Guilt- you might feel like you failed because you think you did not persist enough ("Did I try hard enough?")
You might feel like your body has let you down.
Anger or betrayal- The health system is flawed and does not offer enough support in the early days ("Why didn't anyone help me sooner?")
Confusion ("Why was this so hard when it's supposed to be 'natural'?")
Isolation ("No one seems to understand.")
Shame (I don't want others to know I am formula feeding.)

What helps?

Understanding. When we know why things are not working it is easier to accept.

Validation. It's okay to grieve this. You're mourning something important.

Talking to someone who gets it, a lactation consultant, a therapist, or another mum who's been there.

Honouring your journey. You made choices out of love and courage.

Reframing success. Bonding, nourishing, and loving your baby comes in many forms not just through the breast.

REFERENCES

https://www.breastfeeding.asn.au/resources/breastfeeding-bacteria-and-your-babys-gut

Meta-analysis of effects of exclusive breastfeeding on infant gut microbiota: https://www.nature.com/articles/s41467-018-06473-x?

Shaping the Gut Microbiota by Breastfeeding: https://www.frontiersin.org/journals/pediatrics/articles/10.3389/fped.2019.00047/full?

Comparison of gut microbiota in exclusively breast-fed and formula-fed infants during the first 6 months of life: https://www.nature.com/articles/s41598-020-72635-x?

Gut microbiome and breast-feeding: Implications for early immune development: https://www.jacionline.org/article/S0091-6749%2822%2900992-7/fulltext?

Breastfeeding and the Microbiome: https://www.ohsu.edu/school-of-medicine/moore-institute/breastfeeding-and-microbiome?

Women who breastfeed exhibit cognitive benefits after age 50 https://academic.oup.com/emph/article/9/1/322/6380138

Long-term effects of breastfeeding A SYSTEMATIC REVIEW https://iris.who.int/bitstream/handle/10665/79198/9789241505307_eng.pdf;jsessionid=D8E2F5B54FD2840D47212C24D89C2381?sequence=1

Witkowska-Zimny M, Kaminska-El-Hassan E. Cells of human breast milk. Cell Mol Biol Lett. 2017 Jul 13;22:11. doi: 10.1186/s11658-017-0042-4. PMID: 28717367; PMCID: PMC5508878.

https://www.breastfeeding.asn.au/resources/breastmilk-composition-research
© Australian Breastfeeding Association May 2022 sourced online 15/3/25

SOME TRUSTED ORGANIZATONS

Australian Breastfeeding Association
Pinky MacKay
LCANZ Lactation Consultants Australia and New Zealand
La Leche League International
World Alliance for breastfeeding
Global Breastfeeding Collective

CHAPTER 8
Understanding Emotional Regulation

Romans 12:15 (NIV)
"Rejoice with those who rejoice; mourn with those who mourn."

Colossians 3:12 (NIV)
"Therefore, as God's chosen people, holy and dearly loved, clothe yourselves with compassion, kindness, humility, gentleness and patience."

What is your understanding about emotional regulation? Emotional regulation is basically how we manage and express our emotions in a way that helps us stay balanced. Sometimes, it's a conscious effort like taking deep breaths to calm down after a tough conversation and other times, it happens automatically, like feeling relief after stepping outside for fresh air or patting your cat.

Good emotional regulation helps us handle life's ups and downs without feeling completely overwhelmed or acting on impulse. It's key for mental health, resilience, and maintaining strong relationships. When we struggle with it, though, it can affect our well-being and how we interact with others especially a strong-willed toddler that has no emotional regulation yet.

There are four main parts to healthy emotional regulation:

- Being able to recognise and step back from intense emotions instead of getting swept up in them.
- Finding practical things we that we can do to stop overthinking or dwelling on negative feelings.
- Re-engaging with a situation in a way that's helpful rather than reactive.
- Reframing thoughts from a Biblical perspective.

It's a skill that takes practice, but it's something we all use daily especially in high-stress roles like parenting.

The following are some examples of healthy emotional regulation that you can look for and try:

1. **Reframe the Situation** – *Reframing negative thoughts*- Ask yourself, "What else could be going on here?" This helps shift your perspective and prevent negative assumptions. When faced with a challenging situation, rather than catastrophizing, reframe the event to focus on the learning opportunity. Think "What is this like for my baby?" *This may look like you are thinking your baby is keeping you up and stopping you from*

getting sleep. You know baby cannot manipulate you at this age as cognitively, this area has not developed. You change your thoughts to think "How is baby being impacted?" You then see your baby is really struggling to sleep and need the extra help to calm, regulate and sleep. Something is waking her, I wonder what that could be? Even if you can't work out what it is, remembering when you are upset that just having someone who understands and is present and loving helps you manage it.

2. **Acceptance and mindfulness**- In moments of intense stress, practice acceptance and mindfulness to calm the *nervous system and regain emotional equilibrium. I will surrender to this time. My baby will only need me like this for a short time. I can hear birds and washing machine, I can feel the ground under my feet and the breeze on my face. The great I AM is in this moment, be present with him for a deep breath or two.*

3. **Use Grounding**- Focus on your senses to bring yourself back to the present. *What can I do to calm myself? See- 5 things, Hear- 4 things, Touch- 3 things, Smell- 2 things, Taste- 1 thing. Suck on ice, wash face in cold water.*

4. **Pause and Breathe** – Take a few slow, deep breaths to signal to your body that it's safe to relax. Inhaling deeply through your nose and exhaling slowly can help calm your nervous system. *Breathe deeply slowly in (count to 4) and out (count to 6) 4 times. It really works!*

5. **Move Your Body** – Recognize when an emotion such as anger is escalating. Temporarily remove yourself from the situation to cool down before responding. A quick walk,

stretching, or even shaking out your hands can release built-up tension and help you reset. *Take a break.* A great example of emotional regulation in action! Noticing when emotions like anger are building up and choosing to step away for a moment can prevent reactions we might regret later. Taking a break gives us time to cool down, think clearly, and respond in a way that's more constructive. This is especially important for parents, who often deal with high-pressure situations. A frustrated parent might step away for a few deep breaths before addressing a toddler's tantrum, take a moment to reset after a stressful situation to ensure she provides calm, supportive care. *Put baby somewhere safe and take a breath, drink something, ring someone to come and support you. Then try again once you have calmed.* Often just stepping away gives us time to ask God "What is happening here? What do I need to do? Drinking a cold drink or splash your face with cold water helps too. Put on music and dance a bit!

6. **Express emotions constructively**- Simply identifying what you're feeling ("I'm frustrated," "I feel overwhelmed") can reduce its intensity and make it easier to manage. Use calm, assertive communication to express feelings appropriately instead of bottling them up or lashing out. *It's good for you to talk to your baby, partner family or friends about how you are feeling. I need some help please.*

"Name it to tame it -Dan Siegel". He has many clips on youtube you can watch to understand this more. Essentially when we name the emotion our brains send calming hormones to calm it. God has thought of everything!

7. **Problem-solving-** Instead of ruminating on negative feelings, identify actionable steps to address the root cause of the emotion. What led to this situation? *What can I do differently when faced with this? Why am I feeling this way? Is there anything I can do now to meet this need for me?*

The use of these strategies demonstrates your self-awareness and a proactive approach to managing emotions in healthy and adaptive ways.

CO-REGULATION

What to expect from babies /young children- Babies are born without the ability to regulate. Their brains take years and lots of role modelling from you to learn these skills. All their emotions are valid even the ones that look fake such as fake crying. They don't have the ability to verbalise what they are feeling. Mirroring their expressions can let them know you notice how they are feeling. Babies absorb the emotions in their environment. If you are stressed, they will get stressed. This is why it is so important to be able to manage your emotions well. Recognise your emotions and manage how you respond. Co-regulation is when baby is dysregulated they borrow your calm to regulate. An example of this is when baby wakes and cries, mother comes in and baby stops crying. They see you and their world is ok again.

Tips for when things are getting overwhelming- Pray, put some worship music on, take a break by going out of room and trying some of the above strategies. Call a friend/family for a chat or for them to come over. You can ring a careline. You don't have to face this alone. Name the emotion you are feeling. Lieberman MD discovered when we name the emotions it calms our brain.

Being a mother will be the best thing but also the hardest thing you will ever do. Two great courses you can do are Circle of Security and Tuning into Kids -Gottman

> **Guide to Helping Kids Manage Emotions**
>
> (*Sanya Pelini*)
>
> Children are born with basic emotional reactions (crying, frustration, hunger) but learn complex emotions through social and cultural experiences. The way we respond to their emotions shapes their emotional intelligence.

Remember God is invested in your baby more than you are. He is your refuge.

Psalms 22:9 (TPT)
"Lord, You delivered me safely from my mother's womb.
You are the one who cared for me ever since I was a baby."

Go to him when you are puzzled with what to do.

Psalms 131:2 (TPT)
"I am humbled and quieted in Your presence.
Like a contented child who rests on its mother's lap,
I'm Your resting child and my soul is content in You."

DISCIPLINE- WHAT IS IT?

- TEACH, INSTRUCT, EDUCATE, TRAIN, SCHOOL
- LOVE
- RESOECT
- INTENTIONALITY
- BOUNDARIES AND LIMITS
- GRATITUDE
- GRACE AND FORGIVENESS
- ADAPTABILITY

Let's explore what discipline is and what is it not. From the dictionary there are many meanings of discipline but the one which I will talk about is the one connected with Jesus.

The Root and Meanings of Discipline

Discipline comes from *discipulus,* the Latin word for pupil, which also provided the source of the word disciple (albeit by way of a Late Latin sense-shift to "a follower of Jesus Christ in his lifetime").

TEACH, INSTRUCT, EDUCATE, TRAIN, DISCIPLINE, SCHOOL mean to cause to acquire knowledge or skill. Teach applies to any manner of imparting information or skill so that others may learn. It is not punishment but that does not mean we can't use consequence. We don't learn well when we are fearful.

When we look at Jesus teachings it is through relationship with Him that changes us and causes us to want to follow Him and become more like Him. Children want nothing more than to have love and value in your eyes and to follow you. You are their world. Behaviour is always an indication of an unmet need. What is your child telling you? What is behind their behaviour? What need do they have? How can we be Jesus to our children?

What sort of discipline and freedom did you experience as a child? Was there violence or manipulation? Many families were taught to punish or hit children for children's mistakes or misbehaviour. Children then acted a certain way by fear. This destroys their sense of self and your relationship with them. We now consider any form of physical violence as abuse. Children are just learning. They are learning emotional regulation. They need to learn how to stop doing what they have been told "no" about and be modelled how to distract themselves and move on to other things. How did your parents view mistakes?

Discipline is not punishment as a lot of people think. The phrase *"spare the rod, spoil the child"* doesn't appear exactly in the Bible.

> *Proverbs 13:24 (Message)*
> *"A refusal to correct is a refusal to love;*
> *love your children by disciplining them."*

This verse reminds us that loving our children sometimes means gently correcting them. Letting them do whatever they want may feel kind in the moment, but true love is shown in guiding them toward what is good and right. Thoughtful discipline, done with care and kindness, helps our children grow in wisdom, confidence, and character. Babies/toddlers don't have language but do have more understanding than we give them credit for.

Any emotion is an opportunity to connect with your child. Learning how to help your child recognise their emotions and validate their feelings is paramount to success. Discussions about boundaries and discipline need to be done in the calm and not the heat of the moment.

Hebrews 12:6, 10;
"The Lord disciplines the one He loves, and He chastens everyone He accepts as His son. . . . God disciplines us for our good, in order that we may share in His holiness"

Proverbs 3:12 (CEV)
the Lord corrects everyone He loves,
just as parents correct a child they dearly love.

Proverbs 3:12 (Message)
It's the child He loves that God corrects;
a father's delight is behind all this.

God purposefully corrects us when we make mistakes, and places us in situations that we can use for spiritual development.

These passages indicate that a loving father, especially God takes an active role in the growth of a child (us) and we can do this for our children.

Ephesians 6:4 (Message)
"Fathers, don't frustrate your children with no-win scenarios. Take them by the hand and lead them in the way of the Master."

It is good to reflect on all these things mentioned in this chapter. Discuss them with your partner and pray about them. Teaching can only be done in the calm not in the craziness of the meltdown moment.

The **"fight, flight, freeze, or fright"** response refers to the **body's automatic reaction to perceived danger or stress**. It's part of our survival instinct, governed by the **autonomic nervous system**, especially the **sympathetic nervous system**.

Fight – The body prepares to confront the threat (e.g., clenching fists, increased aggression).

Flight – The urge to escape the danger (e.g., running away, avoiding confrontation).

Freeze – Becoming still or numb, as if "playing dead" (e.g., feeling stuck or paralysed).

Fright – A state of overwhelming fear or shock, where the mind may go blank or dissociate.

These responses happen **automatically and quickly**, often before we even think, to **protect us from harm**. If your child or you are in flight, fright, fight or freeze mode they are not in a state to learn and you are not in a state to teach them. Wait for the calm then talk it out quietly.

> Lord we come to You now and ask for You to guide us in this amazing but complicated journey. It is made simpler by Your guidance and direction. We know You love us and our children. Thank You that we don't have to do this on our own.

WHAT ARE THE 7 TRAITS OF EFFECTIVE PARENTING? (FAMILY FIRST WEBSITE)

The following are seven traits that are often present in the lives of parents who are raising kids who thrive in challenging situations. Parents may excel in some of these areas and fall short in others, but each trait can transform our Christian parenting, filling our children's hearts and minds with God's truth and bringing wisdom into our homes.

LOVE

John the apostle tells us that we learn love by looking at the love God has shown us. God's love came first, and it is a truly sacrificial love.

> *1 John 4:10*
> *"In this is love, not that we have loved God but that He loved us and sent His Son to be the propitiation for our sins"*

Do you know what you love? Look at the people, activities and things you're attached to. Look at the sacrifices you make to see those people, do those activities or use those things. These are the areas of your life where you love. Children can see where your priorities are, where your love is directed.

God's love helps parents counteract our natural selfishness. His love reveals itself in His commitment to us and His sacrifice for us, long after our emotions have faded away. Children learn God's love through the sacrificial commitments we make to them and teach them to make.

RESPECT

The apostle Paul writes that we should think like Christ and treat others as more important than ourselves Respect recognizes the best in people. It is more than acknowledging a child's accomplishments. Children and teens are worthy of respect because God created them and loves them.

> *Philippians 2:4 (MSG)*
> *"Put yourself aside, and help others get ahead.*
> *Don't be obsessed with getting your own advantage.*
> *Forget yourselves long enough to lend a helping hand."*

Respect teaches us not to treat others as unimportant. Nothing hurts a child more than being treated as if he is useless, and almost nothing encourages him more than being respected and valued.

One way to show respect to your family is to watch your language. Biblical parenting outlines specific principles involving use of language within a family. Refuse to use cruel language whether directed toward family members in your home or outsiders. As Christian parents, our language habits really do influence our ability to model respect to our children.

INTENTIONALITY

Being Intentional means talking about and living out our values and priorities before allowing other influences into our home. This trait nurtures a consistency in family life that reinforces the other traits. When parents are intentional, they grow in wisdom and are able to keep their focus on how they act as believing parents.

> *Colossians 1:12*
> *"It is strength that endures the unendurable and spills over into joy, thanking the Father who makes us strong enough to take part in everything bright and beautiful that He has for us."*

It is easy to be passive and let media and other influences set our family's priorities, but it's more effective to pay careful attention to *how* we live our lives. This is intentionality: making decisions as parents about how we will own the spiritual atmosphere in our homes.

BOUNDARIES AND LIMITS

Dr. Henry Cloud and Dr. John Townsend, authors of the "Boundaries" book series, write that the purpose of boundaries in biblical parenting to "let good things in and keep bad things out." Ordering our home with healthy boundaries for kids and adults helps us do that.

> *Hebrews 12:1 (NKJV)*
> *"Therefore we also, since we are surrounded by so great a cloud of witnesses, let us lay aside every weight, and the sin which so easily ensnares us, and let us run with endurance the race that is set before us,"*

Being deliberate about boundaries around media, behaviour, relationships, godly living and a vibrant faith means we do not let culture determine what is healthy for our family.

> *Proverbs 14:7*
> *"Leave the presence of a fool,*
> *for there you do not meet words of knowledge"*

If we don't set our own boundaries in our families, other influences culture, extended family or trends will set our children's moral boundaries, and we may become surprised and dismayed by what they have learned.

GRATITUDE

As Paul begins his letter to the Philippians, he tells them how thankful he is every time he thinks of them. Gratitude is not just a polite reaction to something good. It is a cultivated habit and a vital part of healthy relationships.

> *Philippians 1:3-4 (MSG)*
> *Every time you cross my mind;*
> *I break out in exclamations of thanks to God.*
> *Each exclamation is a trigger to prayer.*
> *I find myself praying for you with a glad heart.*

When we practice gratitude in our families, it helps children and parents fight selfishness, which causes division among families and friends. When gratitude is expressed on a regular basis and in deliberate ways, it helps our children learn to see all the good God does in our lives. A natural outcome of this within biblical parenting is that we learn to naturally praise Him, regardless of how we feel in the moment.

GRACE AND FORGIVENESS

Grace and forgiveness shock us. God forgave us while we were still sinners. He shows grace to imperfect people and continues to involve them in His plan.

Christian parents need to be willing to model forgiveness and grace to their children, regardless of the personal cost. Human nature prevents us from easily giving grace and forgiveness, yet we learn from God's Word that we need to give both or we can't expect to be forgiven.

Matthew 6:14-15 (MSG)
"In prayer there is a connection between what God does and what you do.
You can't get forgiveness from God,
for instance, without also forgiving others.
If you refuse to do your part, you cut yourself off from God's part."

ADAPTABILITY

While he was in prison, Paul said something amazing:

Philippians 4:11 (ESV)
"I have learned in whatever situation I am to be content"

Paul learned to find peace in Christ, despite his situation. His personal happiness was not attached to his position, how well he was doing or what he was doing.

Teaching adaptability helps our children find peace, a deep peace that is stronger than the stresses and trials of life. Peace counteracts the unproductive worry that causes us to lose our trust in God. This flexibility and resilience, grown in difficult circumstances, allows a family to face both hardships and joys together, as they grow deeper in their faith.

REFERENCES

"Discipline." Merriam-Webster.com Dictionary, Merriam-Webster, https://www.merriam-webster.com/dictionary/discipline. Accessed 3 Feb. 2025.

Downloaded and adapted from https://positivepsychology.com/emotion-regulation/ and adapted on 29/1/25 9 Jan 2025 by *Susan McGarvie, Ph.D.*

(*Sanya Pelini*) https://www.gottman.com/blog/age-age-guide-helping-kids-manage-emotions/

The Circle of Security program is parent/child psychotherapy designed to assist parents to provide their children with the emotional support needed to develop secure attachment, resilience and enhanced school readiness. Circle of security https://circleofsecuritynetwork.org/the_circle_of_security.html

Tuning in to Kids is a suite of parenting programs that focuses on strengthening the connection between parents/caregivers and their kids. When kids and parents develop skills in effectively communicating about emotions, family relationships are stronger https://tuningintokids.org.au/parents/

What are the 7 Traits of Effective Parenting? Downloaded and adapted from Focus on the family website 25/5/25

Dr. Henry Cloud and Dr. John Townsend, authors of the "Boundaries"

Lieberman MD, Eisenberger NI, Crockett MJ, Tom SM, Pfeifer JH, Way BM. Putting feelings into words: affect labeling disrupts amygdala activity in response to affective stimuli. Psychol Sci. 2007 May;18(5):421-8. doi: 10.1111/j.1467-9280.2007.01916.x. PMID: 17576282.

CHAPTER 9

What makes a positive birthing experience?

John 16:21 (NIV)
"A woman giving birth to a child has pain because her time has come; but when her baby is born she forgets the anguish because of her joy that a child is born into the world."

CREATING A POSITIVE BIRTH EXPERIENCE.

Women birth differently. Women perceive pain differently. Every woman's birthing journey is unique, yet both research and the voices of mothers reveal several consistent themes that contribute to a deeply positive experience. It's less about how the birth unfolds or even the pain felt and more about how a woman *feels* during and after the experience.

WHAT MAKES A POSITIVE BIRTHING EXPERIENCE?

For women of faith, there's an added source of strength. God is intimately involved in both you and your baby's lives. If you invite Him into this journey, He will guide and sustain you. Trusting His presence and staying attuned to His promptings during birth can offer a sense of peace and confidence that transcends the circumstances. His peace truly can lead you every step of the way.

BIRTH IS A TIME OF TRANSITION

Time	Time to allow baby to open up places that have not been open before
Time	Time for you to work towards new role as parents
Time	Time to prepare you for the emotional journey of being a parent
Allow	Allow yourself to be peaceful in that time

Women are stronger than we know, and we are designed to give birth. Our bodies have been uniquely designed to help baby move and make a way through the birth passage. The more we find out about the intricacies of our bodies and those of our baby the more it points to our Creator. He will be with you throughout this amazing journey. It takes a while, as muscles are worked harder than ever before, and ligaments give and make space. Bones of your pelvis can shift and change shape to allow baby to move through tight spaces. If it happens too quickly then the woman and baby is often in shock. Embrace the slowness of birth and surrender to its process, embrace the unknown and trust your Maker.

Labour is hard but can be helped by an atmosphere of quiet and privacy dim lighting and little conversation, and no expectation of rationality from the labouring woman. Under these conditions a woman will intuitively choose the movements, sounds, breathing, and positions that will birth her baby most easily. There is no right way. Hospital environments and routines are not generally conducive to the shift in consciousness that giving birth naturally requires. Stay home as long as you can in your safe place.

Music is powerful, it reaches into our soul and connects us with the Holy Spirit. Play songs that calm your spirit and connect you with our triune God. He is your power source.

Keywords

- God designed me to do this!
- My cervix is opening.
- It's a muscle working.
- My baby is moving down.
- I can do all thing through Christ who gives me strength.
- My baby is safe in His hands.
- This is a healthy pain.
- I am strong.
- Listen to partner countdown (10, 9, 8, 7.......).
- Find verses to quote to remind you God is with you.

How to give yourself the best chance

1. Gentle exercise/ Good diet throughout pregnancy

2. Research the course (know what to expect). Do some sort of birthing course there are so many to choose from. Knowledge is power.

3. Start to plan and practice relaxation/ distraction. These might include dancing, worshipping and prayer. Don't be shy in front of staff. You may give them a window into your walk with Jesus, planting seeds in their life.

4. Find the right support people. This is your time, and you get to say who is there and who is not.

5. Try different things, be open.

6. Rest/ Sleep when you can.

7. Continue to eat light diet and water during the birth.

8. Stay relaxed.

CHARACTERISTICS OF A CALMING SUPPORT PERSON

Calm in a crisis.

Always positive.

Loves you.

Makes you feel safe and comfortable.

Intuitive to your feelings and needs.

Nurturing.

Good attitude to birth, with no personal baggage (past negative experiences).

The journey is about teamwork so having support people that get you, love you and are calm is vital.

The role of the support person is vital in this time.

They are there to:

- Help you relax.
- Keep you focussed.
- Be present (not on their phone).
- Advocate for you with staff at hospital.
- Remind you of your goal.
- Keep you hydrated.
- Help you breathe, dance, find joy in the process.

Components of the Birth Process

The powers- contractions

The passages- bony structures and tissues

The passenger- the baby

I think it's important to believe in the design of your body by our magnificent Father. This helps you to trust the process. It will help in remaining calm and focussed on your part.

WHAT MAKES A POSITIVE BIRTHING EXPERIENCE?

Good pain relief in labour is not the same as a perception of personal control or satisfaction in childbirth. In other words, you may have significant pain during the birth but feel in control during the process and have great satisfaction afterward. On the other hand, you might have total pain relief during the birth but feel totally out of control and unhappy about your experience when it is over.

Here are some of the key elements that often shape a positive birth experience:

1. **Feeling heard and respected**

    When women are listened to, have their preferences acknowledged, and are included in decisions, they often feel more empowered regardless of whether the birth is natural, assisted, or surgical. Many mothers say that being respected and supported during labour made all the difference in how they remember their birth.

2. **Emotional and physical support.**

    Having someone by your side, whether a partner, doula, midwife, or trusted friend can ease fear and foster a sense of safety. Gentle touch, movement, breathing techniques, and encouraging words can help you feel calm and cared for. Mothers often recall that simply having a supportive, steady presence helped them stay grounded and focused.

3. **Being included in and informed about choices and autonomy.**

    Understanding your options and being actively involved in decisions builds confidence. Even when plans change, feeling informed and respected helps you stay in control of your experience. Women frequently share that being part of the decision-making process gave them a sense of empowerment, even in unpredictable moments.

4. **A calm and safe environment.**

    The atmosphere during birth matters. Soft lighting, soothing music, familiar objects, and gentle voices can create a peaceful space that supports relaxation and progress. Many mothers found that a calm, supportive environment helped them feel safer and more in tune with their body during labour.

5. **Compassionate, competent care.**

    Care that honours both your physical, spiritual and emotional needs is essential. How you're treated by your birth team often leaves a lasting impression, even more than the events themselves. Women often remember the kindness, reassurance, and skill of their caregivers long after the birth.

6. **Time to reflect and process.**

    After birth, having the opportunity to talk through your experience especially if it didn't go as expected can support healing and emotional well-being. Many new mothers say that sharing their birth story with a compassionate listener helped them feel peace, validation, and pride.

In summary: A positive birth experience is grounded in feeling safe, respected, supported, and empowered no matter how your baby arrives. It is grounded in faith that you don't do it alone and who better to support you than the great designer Himself.

HOW TO WORK WITH YOUR HORMONES IN LABOR.

God designed your body to give birth, and your hormones are there to help every step of the way. Trusting the process and creating a supportive environment can make a big difference! Working *with* your hormones rather than against them can make birth smoother and more manageable. Here are some practical ways to support each hormone during birth. Hormones are like the body's natural birth team, working behind the scenes to help things progress smoothly. Each one has a specific role, and together, they create the rhythm of birth.

Here's how they work:

Boosting Oxytocin (The Love Hormone).

Oxytocin is the driving force behind birth! It's the hormone responsible for contractions and helps labour move along. It's released when you feel safe, supported, and loved so dim lights, gentle touch, and calm surroundings can boost it. *It's job is to keep your uterus working, encouraging it to contract and bring your baby closer to you!* Oxytocin makes contractions strong and effective, so you want plenty of it flowing!

Stay calm and connected – Hug, kiss, or hold hands with your partner. Eye contact and loving words can boost oxytocin.

Create a cozy environment – Dim lights, soft music, and familiar scents can help. Think of what makes you feel safe and relaxed.

Gentle touch and movement – Massage, skin-to-skin contact, and rhythmic movement (like swaying or rocking) encourage oxytocin release.

Laugh and feel loved – Watch a funny video, listen to a comforting voice, or surround yourself with people who make you feel good.

Avoid stress or interruptions – Loud voices, too many questions, fear, too many people, or a rushed atmosphere can lower oxytocin levels and slow labour down. You get to say who is in your birthing room. If too many people ask some to leave.

Encouraging Endorphins: God's Pain Relief!

As contractions intensify, your body releases endorphins these are natural painkillers that help you cope with labour. When oxytocin and endorphins work together, they create a flow that helps you stay focused and even experience moments of euphoria. *Have you heard about women feeling "in the zone" during labour? That's the power of endorphins!* Endorphins help you cope with contractions and even create a sense of euphoria.

Deep, steady breathing – Slow exhales help keep you in control and reduce pain perception.

Use water – A warm bath or shower can increase endorphins and help you relax between contractions.

Positive affirmations – Repeating calming phrases ("I am strong, I am safe, my baby is coming, God's in control") can help shift your focus.

Rhythmic movement – Walking, swaying, dancing and rocking on a birth ball can boost endorphins naturally.

Avoid fear and tension – If you feel overwhelmed, find ways to reset—change positions, dim the lights, or ask for reassurance from your support team.

Keeping Adrenaline: The Stress Hormone Low.

Adrenaline is released when you feel scared or anxious. It's your fight, flight or freeze hormone. Too much of it can *slow* labour down because it blocks oxytocin. That's why a calm and reassuring environment is so important, when you feel safe, your body can focus on birthing rather than responding to stress. *This is why bright lights, loud voices, or feeling rushed can make labour stall it's your body trying to protect you from "danger," even when there isn't any!* Adrenaline can stall labour if it gets too high. The goal is to stay as relaxed and confident as possible.

Stay in a familiar, calm space – Feeling safe reduces adrenaline.

Use low lighting and quiet voices – This keeps the birth environment peaceful and oxytocin flowing.

Trust your body and the process – If fears creep in, remind yourself that your body knows what to do. Quote verses to remind you how much God loves you and is with you.

Limit distractions – Too many people in the room, constant talking, or interruptions can make labour feel stressful.

Avoid feelings of fear or pressure – If something doesn't feel right, ask for reassurance or request changes to your environment.

Encouraging Prolactin: The Nurturing Hormone (The Bonding Hormone).

Right after birth, prolactin kicks in to support breastfeeding and bonding with your baby. It helps with milk production and makes you feel more connected to your newborn. *It's God's way of helping you and your baby transition into this new chapter together.*

Immediate skin-to-skin contact – Holding your baby against your chest right after birth helps prolactin surge. Stay this way for a couple of hours.

Dim, warm environment – Babies adjust best to life outside the womb when the environment is calm and quiet.

Let baby lead the first few feeds – Many newborns instinctively find the breast when given time and support.

Your hormones work best when you feel **safe, supported, and in control of your birth space**. Surround yourself with people who encourage you, minimize stress, and trust your body's God given natural process.

What is birth like for your baby?

The Home

Imagine a snug warm wet space where every movement is restricted and every sound gets to you through fluid, muffled, gentle. There is your mothers heartbeat strong and regular, reassuring, then your placenta faster but also constant. Over them is a noise that comes and goes; a gentle murmuring both one lower and a second sound higher. Sometimes your world is intruded on by pokes and sounds that are very loud. Then there is a gentle rolling that happens for a period then stillness. There is something you poke often when you hear his voice. From time to time your world gets squeezed for a short time. As time goes on your world gets smaller and smaller, less room to move. You don't have to get up to get a drink you just drink and wee there where you are, you have your own food line, nothing to do except suck your thumb! Sounds appealing to some!

WHAT MAKES A POSITIVE BIRTHING EXPERIENCE?

> The Journey
>
> One day something changed, your world started to squeeze you tighter and tighter. Then it was pushing you down against the wall of your space. This seemed to go on forever. It is no use fighting it. It is a force like you have never known before. Then the wall seemed to give a bit, and you are being pushed through this very tight space!
>
> The change
>
> Then all the sudden it gave way, and you were out in bright lights and many voices then cold wind and touch. It felt very different and strange, and you open your mouth and cry for the first time. It takes you by surprise as you breathe in your first breath.
>
> Your mother's heartbeat is gone; everything is strange then you are placed up on your mother's chest and that heartbeat is there again and that soothing voice you open your eyes blinking to see your mother. Then the lower voice is there too, you turn to look straight into the eyes of your father. His calm hand is soothing helping you with this momentous change. Everything in your world is different, your one anchor are those familiar voices, your mother's smell and heartbeat.

It takes a while to adjust to the change, you cry when you become overwhelmed. Your mother and father are there to help you adjust with calming hands and voices. Together you will get through.

> Sometimes birth doesn't go as planned, you may feel disappointed or distressed. It is important to have the opportunity to

debrief birth if you need it. Find someone who is trained to listen and talk through the experience.

Contemplate these things:

- What was it like for you?
- What was it like for baby?
- What was it like for Dad?
- Get some help if you need it.

CHAPTER 10
Baby Cues and Sleep

Neuroscience has now shown us the more involved we are with baby's care the more in tune we are to baby's needs. It changes our brain to be more empathetic. Each time we look into our baby's eyes a million neural connections happen both in our baby's brain and in our brain. The more time you spend caring for your baby the more this happens. This is God's way of you becoming more protective, loving and in tune with your baby and develop a sixth sense of their needs. Scientists now call this *parent-child synchrony*. By you providing gentle, loving, responsive care your baby is learning how to trust.

Baby cues are the ways babies tell us their needs before they can talk. It's much easier to follow their cues than try to make your baby follow a routine. If you watch your baby closely you will start to pick up what they do when they have a need, whether it's food, rest, comfort, or stimulation. They are subtle signals using body language, facial expressions, sounds, and movements. Understanding your baby's cues helps you to respond sensitively, which builds trust and supports healthy development. There are lots of books about babies in general but none about your specific baby. Although most babies have similar cues you will write your babies own book with their cues. My granddaughter from early on would lean towards me when I was standing close. One time in church my daughter was trying to help her sleep in her arms, and she kept leaning towards me. As soon as she was in my arms she fell straight to sleep. She was only about 6 weeks at the time.

1. Hunger Cues.

Babies are born with tummies that have not ever digested anything but liquor. They practice swallowing and the pass urine back into the same liquor. This liquor was thought to be sterile but now we know it has some beneficial bacteria in it. Babies often show signs of hunger *before* crying, which is a late cue.

Look for:

Early hunger cues:

- Smacking or licking lips
- Sucking on fingers, hands, or rooting (turning head with mouth open)
- Leaning towards your breast

- Squirming

Mid hunger cues:

- Becoming more active or fidgety
- Trying to move toward the breast or bottle
- Clenched fists

Late hunger cues:

- Crying, turning red, or getting frantic.

(It's best to feed before this stage if possible.)

We often don't go very long without wanting a drink or snack. Keep this in mind when you think your baby is hungry. Babies have little tummies. Why then should we expect longer periods between snacks, after all they can't go to the fridge.

2. Tired Cues

These help you spot when your baby is ready to sleep. One of the first signs to look for is staring off or looking glazed. They may start to yawn or rub their eyes or ears. Losing interest in people or play, becoming fussy or clingy baby's movements might become jerky. Some babies have a tired squawk or look flushed around eyebrows.

Baby will only be awake for a short time maybe 1 hr at first. This only allows time to feed, change your baby and maybe get some face-to-face time. Sleep is vital for babies, a time to grow and process their awake time. Sleep is one of the hardest things to predict. We sleep differently every night even as adults. Babies need to wake frequently to feed and when they wake, they will need you to show them their world is still ok. Mothers stress about sleep, as it's so hard to function without it. Many people spend a lot of time and effort trying to work out how to get their baby to sleep more. Newborns especially need to feed and sleep. This may be on you or in their safe sleep space.

You need to sleep where and when you can. Babies sleep is not a given so know that baby will do more than eat and sleep on a schedule. If they are tired help them sleep, even if it's on you. Contact napping is something most mothers do when they need to, to ensure their baby is getting enough rest. If they look hungry feed them. In between try to do what you need to, including sleep for you. Babies initially are not awake for long periods. Babies that are overtired are harder to get to sleep and often won't sleep well.

3. Overstimulation Cues

Babies can get overwhelmed by too much light, noise, or handling. Signs could include looking away, turning head or body away. Some babies stiffen or arch their back, splaying fingers. Some babies will just fuss or cry. Some will scream as though they are in pain.

4. Need for Connection or Comfort

When babies are born their world becomes disorganised and they need you to comfort them often. This comfort comes in the form of your heartbeat, your smell, your voice, music, movement and breastmilk! These are your baby's anchors in an uncertain world. Babies also cue when they want closeness by making eye contact, reaching out arms, making cooing sounds. Smiling or moving toward your voice are early cues but sometimes when you don't notice they will just cry. If you are separated at birth from your baby, they will find it hard to be separated at home. All babies benefit from being held more. You just can't spoil a baby.

5. Pain

It is hard to tell when your baby is in pain or just uncomfortable. They cry to let you know they need your help. Some babies cry a lot and some don't. If you are worried it doesn't hurt to get them checked. Breastmilk has pain relieving properties in it so if all else fails offer them the breast.

6. Need for a Break

Sometimes, babies just need a pause, you might notice sneezing or hiccupping (not always but often a sign of too much stimulation), yawning or rubbing eyes (also overlaps with tiredness), arching back or squirming away from touch.

Baby cues matter because responding to cues helps your baby build trust and security. They know you are there when they need you. It supports emotional development and helps them feel safe. It prevents unnecessary crying or distress. Calm babies feed and sleep better and strengthens the parent-baby bond. Connection is their main need in life, it helps them feel understood and accepted.

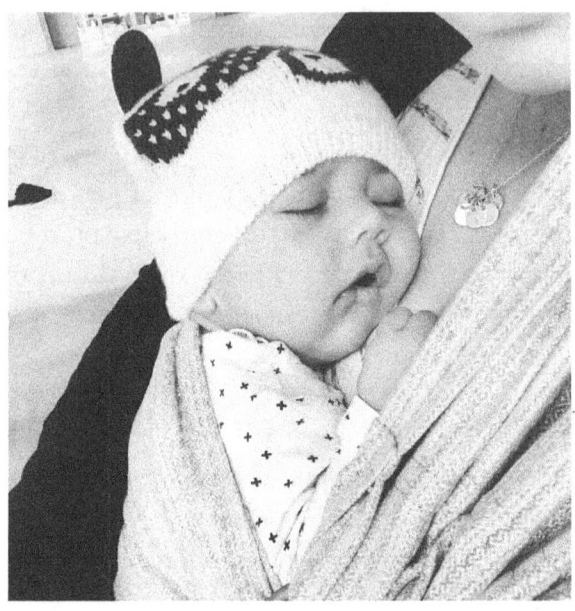

"Birth suddenly disrupts the baby's organization developed in womb. During the months following birth, baby tries to regain his sense of organization and fit into life outside the womb. Birth and adaptation to postnatal life bring out the temperament of the baby, so for the first time he must do something to have his needs met. His natural response is to cry to let you know." If hungry, cold, or startled, he cries. He must try to get the things he needs from his care giving environment. If his needs are simple and he can get what he wants easily, he's labelled an "easy baby"; if he does not adapt readily, he is labelled "difficult."" – Dr. William Sears.(adapted)

It is difficult for the mother when a baby cries a lot in these times but it's important to reframe this from baby is difficult to he/she is having a hard time.

The "Nurture Revolution" sleep approach, spearheaded by Dr. Greer Kirshenbaum, challenges traditional sleep training methods by emphasizing nurturing care and responding to a baby's cues. It rejects the idea of letting babies cry it out and instead advocates for co-regulation, safe bedsharing (with proper precautions), and responding to night wakings to support healthy brain development.

Key Principles of the Nurture Revolution Sleep Approach:

Rejection of Cry-It-Out:

This approach explicitly opposes sleep training methods that involve letting babies cry without comfort.

Nurturing Co-regulation:

It emphasizes the importance of responding to a baby's needs, including night wakings, to help them regulate their emotions and develop a secure attachment.

Safe Bedsharing and Contact Sleep:

Kirshenbaum advocates for safe bedsharing or using a sidecar crib, especially for babies who need physical closeness to feel secure.

Following Baby's Cues:

Parents are encouraged to be attuned to their baby's sleep cues and needs, rather than adhering to rigid schedules.

Brain-Building Sleep:

The approach highlights how nurturing interactions during sleep, such as cuddling and responding to needs, can positively impact the developing brain.

How it differs from traditional sleep training:

Traditional sleep training often involves techniques like the Ferber method (gradual extinction) or the cry-it-out method, which encourage babies to self-soothe and fall asleep independently, potentially involving periods of crying. The Nurture Revolution, on the other hand, focuses on responding to the baby's needs and fostering a secure attachment, believing that nurturing care is essential for healthy brain development.

In essence, The Nurture Revolution suggests that:

- Comforting a baby to sleep (with breastfeeding, rocking, cuddling, etc.) is not a bad habit, but a form of nurturing.
- Night waking is a normal part of infant development and should be responded to with empathy and care.
- Babies are not capable of self-soothing in the same way adults are and need co-regulation, particularly during sleep.
- Nurturing experiences during sleep contribute to a baby's emotional resilience and mental well-being.

    (Summarized by AI)

Sleep is one of those areas that mothers often struggle with. This is why we need our village.

- Sleep is so important to us as human beings. Sleep allows the brain and body to slow down and engage in processes of recovery, promoting better physical and mental performance the next day and over the long-term. This is why we struggle with less sleep. Babies grow while sleeping. When they get enough sleep, they feed better, are more able to cope with wake times and can go to sleep easier. If your baby will only sleep on you then this is more important than cleaning the house.

- What happens when you don't sleep is that these fundamental processes are short-circuited, affecting thinking, concentration, energy levels, and mood. Mothers need to manage often with disturbed sleep. This is a difficult adjustment.

- If you are stressed or your home is stressed, then you can expect this to effect baby's mental state and sleep as well. If this is an ongoing problem, it is important to seek some help. Look for strategies to work on this and bring in your support people.

- Babies are born with an immature nervous system. Babies need to borrow your calm to regulate their emotions so need you to be calm for this to happen. This is especially so when they are falling asleep. As babies are adjusting to being outside the womb your voice, smell, arms, heartbeat and movement help them stay calm. They feel safe in your arms.

- Children bounce off stress and need a calm environment to flourish.

SLEEP CYCLE DURATION, BRAIN DEVELOPMENT AND PATTERNS

Quiet sleep. As they grow up, their active sleep cycles will reduce and they will have more quiet sleep. During quiet sleep, they won't move much at all and might be difficult to rouse. This is also called deep sleep. You can transition them from car to bassinet well when in this stage.

Active sleep: You might notice that your baby has quite a lot of active (or dream) sleep. All young babies have more active sleep than older babies and children. Active sleep is when they move their arms and legs, suck and even smile. This might be confusing, but it doesn't mean they are awake. Newborns spend about 50% of their sleep in active sleep (REM sleep), which is crucial for brain development. This phase is associated with increased brain activity and is believed to support neural growth and cognitive development. They may move and grizzle in this stage of sleep. They process their development in this stage so when they are starting to roll, they may roll in their sleep. When they are learning to talk, they may talk. This may wake them up.

Transitional state. At the end of active sleep, your baby usually stirs as they move into a transitional state and it seems as if they might be awake. This is when they might cry and call out. Sometimes they will manage to go back to sleep, other times they will need your help. Take a deep breath here and wait for the second or ongoing call from them, they may just go back to sleep.

Environmental Factors: Mothers have often found that napping in environments with ambient noise, like near a washing machine, may help babies sleep and differentiate between day and night, potentially leading to better nighttime sleep.

Australian Breastfeeding association website explains sleep this way.

How long is a baby sleep cycle?

During the first three months of your baby's life, their newborn sleep cycle is only just starting to develop. Your new baby may sleep for 14–17 hours a day with periods of sleep for as little as 50 minutes to two hours of sleep, at any time of the day and night.

On average, sleep cycles of active and quiet sleep last about 50 minutes, although sometimes can be as short as 30–40 minutes.

Sleep patterns appear, disappear or change as a baby grows from newborn to older baby to toddler. The actual pattern of sleeping and waking varies widely from baby to baby, just as it does in older children and adults. During the first 2 to 3 years, sleep patterns can appear to 'go backwards' at times. Some people call this a 'regression'. It's normal and isn't caused by anything that you are doing or not doing.

There are two types of sleep – light sleep and deep sleep. Very young babies need to conserve energy to grow, so they usually sleep a lot. They spend about 60% of their sleep in light sleep.[1] This helps baby's brain to grow and also lets them wake often to make sure they are fed.

Breastfed babies wake more easily from active sleep than formula-fed babies. You may be told this is a bad thing but in fact, it's good. It may be one of the reasons why breastfed babies have a lower risk of Sudden Infant Death Syndrome (SIDS).[2]

As your baby grows, they will spend less time in light sleep and more time in deep sleep.

Why do babies wake?

There are many reasons why your baby may wake during the night. Sometimes you might be able to work it out, many times you won't. It can also be for several reasons:

In the early days, babies have no idea about day and night.

Young babies have tiny tummies which need to be refilled frequently. Short night feeds can send your baby (and you) back to sleep very quickly.

You may be told that your baby isn't sleeping or has started to wake again, because they are hungry or because you don't have enough milk. There are many reasons for babies to start waking. Solutions such as formula top-ups and early starting of solids are sometimes suggested but may make no difference and even make the situation worse.

Babies are easily disturbed. Too hot, too cold, some prefer to be wrapped firmly, others prefer to have arms and legs free. Some babies wake with the slightest noise, others wake when it's too quiet.

Some babies and toddlers who have been sleeping well for weeks or even months, start to wake again. They might be going through a phase, perhaps they've learned to roll over and that wakes them. Rather than try to return them to their previous sleeping pattern, it's probably less stressful to wait for the stage to settle down.

Some babies are noisy sleepers. You may hear them wakening but if you wait a bit, they may actually put themselves back to sleep.

> Babies need sleep to grow and develop well. But babies' sleep needs vary, just as the sleep needs of older children and adults do. Your baby might be doing well with more or less sleep than other babies the same age.
>
> Your baby's mood and wellbeing is often a good guide to whether your baby is getting enough sleep.
>
> If your baby is:
>
> - wakeful and grizzly, they might need more sleep
> - wakeful and contented, they're probably getting enough sleep.

You might have heard of sleep training. What is extinction/controlled crying?

- Desperate parents often try controlled crying.

- The worst thing about control crying is that it depends on the parent disconnecting from responding to the baby's needs instinctually as they want to. If you respond to your baby lovingly in the daytime but are unavailable at night it confuses them, they do not feel safe.

- Control Crying works on the basis that baby's give up calling out as they realise that no one is coming. This breaks their trust.

- Often babies get more and more distressed. parents get distressed as well. This increases cortisol that stays in baby's system for hours after.

- They often respond with flight, fight or freeze.

REFERENCES

"The Nurture Revolution" by Greer Kirshenbaum

Australian Breastfeeding Association https://www.breastfeeding.asn.au/resources/understanding-baby-sleep

Leclere, C., Viaux, S., Avril, M., et al. (2014). Why synchrony matters during mother-child interactions: A systematic review. *PLoS One, 9*(12), e113571.

Evans, C. A., & Porter, C. L. (2009). The emergence of mother-infant co-regulation during the first year: Links to infants' developmental status and attachment. *Infant Behavior and Development, 32*(2), 147-158.

Swain, J. E. (2011). Becoming a parent: Biobehavioral and brain science perspectives. *Current Problems in Pediatric and Adolescent Health Care, 41*(7), 192-196.

Baker, B., & McGrath, J. M. (2011). Maternal-infant synchrony: An integrated review of the literature. *Neonatal Paediatric and Child Health Nursing, 14*(3), 2-13.

CHAPTER 11

The New You

Proverbs 31:25-26 (NIV)
"She is clothed with strength and dignity;
she can laugh at the days to come.
She speaks with wisdom, and faithful instruction is on her tongue."

It's time to look at what you think motherhood will look like. All the movies either make it look easy or make you laugh at how hard it is. I feel they portray an illusion, that is not realistic. None of them can help us to sit in the loneliness that most of us feel at some stage. Motherhood is often messy and loud. I often have met pregnant women who have started a university course for when they bring a baby home thinking they will have 3-4 hours between feeds to do it. They think that because they won't be going to work, they will have time. Babies are a fulltime job and one that does not allow for lunch breaks, weekends or holidays. Getting time for a shower or toilet is an art that you will perfect in time, most days. It is all consuming, unrelenting, magnificent and life changing.

Despite this it's the most important and best job you will ever have. It changes us from a person consumed with life from our own perspective to someone who puts the needs of our child first.

Babies have a way of reaching into your soul and changing you. You will be more focussed on the things that matter. It changes everything. You have probably already noticed you are quicker to cry. I remember my daughter 30 weeks pregnant hit a bird with her car. She cried so much and found it difficult to forget about it. Although always compassionate and caring towards all animals, God was developing a new level of compassion that she would need as a mother.

Research has now found that when women are pregnant, parts of your baby's cells cross the placenta to your blood and leave remnants of their cells in your system. These stem cells can gravitate to where mother needs healing. We still have so much to learn. God's design is intricate. We know our brain changes. Ultrasounds show changes in the brain from before pregnancy to after. This is so you can focus on baby rather than external issues. It's a time where we need to bond with our baby and be their advocate in life. The more that you watch and care for your baby the quicker you will pick up their cues and that will help guide you. From pregnancy you are the expert on your baby. You are still learning but you know more than doctors or midwives about your baby. You have them growing inside your body. I remember watching Sister Act movie while pregnant with Kelsie. She jumped around every time the music came on. She still has that love of music.

Can you keep an open mind about what it will be like as a mother? Fall in love with your baby no matter who she or he is and what they will become. They are loved with the deepest love available from their heavenly Father. Let Him and them show you how to mother them.

Society will push you to weigh them up by their standards. Is she/he a good baby? I often wonder and respond with "What is a bad baby?" Does she/he sleep well? So much affects sleep. Society wants our babies to eat and sleep so we can do other things. God wants you to respond to your baby with compassion and love no matter what is going on.

Becoming a mother brings a lot of emotional and mental challenges at first, especially around birth, then your new life. Your brain is trying to adapt to all the changes while your body is healing from birth. Over time, handling these ongoing demands can actually help build up your brain's strength and resilience later in life.

I love being a mum but……
I miss parts of my old life.

Such conflicting thoughts and emotions!
Not sure who you can talk to about it?

Sometimes you will feel guilty for even thinking it
The thoughts just go around and around
I wish I was back at work, but I don't want to leave my baby
I am bored and exhausted
I am overjoyed but worried if I should feel this way
I don't know who to talk to.
It ok and perfectly normal to think and feel this way

What emotions are you feeling?

- Close your eyes
- Just concentrate on your breathing
- Take note of your body
- Are there any areas saying notice me?
- Can you isolate any emotions
- Write them down

BECOMING A MUM CHANGES EVERYTHING

As a new mum, I will discover that life takes on a whole new dimension.

I won't always have the final say in what I do, my baby's needs will shape my day. I'll be so needed, so loved, and at times so overwhelmed. The tasks will feel never-ending, and time for myself will be rare. Some days, I'll feel completely disorganized or emotionally stretched. But then my baby will smile… and I'll melt. I'll be reminded that what I'm doing matters deeply, even when it's hard. There will be moments when I feel completely touched out, but also moments of joy I never imagined.

WHAT MAKES IT ALL WORTH IT

I'll find a new sense of purpose in motherhood. Feeling needed, most of the time, will feel fulfilling. The way my baby looks at me will be enough to soften even the hardest day. Their laughter will light up the room and I will laugh so much more. I'll feel deeply loved. I'll know I'm doing something profoundly important. I'll love more fiercely than I ever thought possible.

And I'll learn to find joy in the simple things.

BEFORE BABY – WHO I WAS

Before baby, I was organized, ticking things off gave me a sense of control.

I worked hard, but I still had time for myself. I decided how my day would flow. I could see friends spontaneously, enjoy my hobbies, and plan without interruption. Success felt measurable, a completed to-do list, a project finished, a night out enjoyed. When things got tough, I could walk away, distract myself, or shut down.

After birth, I might find those emotions rising up in ways I hadn't expected.

After birth the things that once helped me cope may no longer fit the same way in this season of life.

What can I do?

- You can still plan your day with flexibility
- Realize that what you are doing in caring for another human being is huge
- Talk to your partner
- Plan date nights.
- Ask yourself what can I still do for me?
- Plan for me time
- Who can help?
- Meet with other mums.

It's important to plan somethings before the baby comes. Talk to your partner about your expectations with care of the baby. He can start to have some baby time without you from early weeks. Start with you having a sleep then work up to going out for coffee. When home from work it will need to be all hands-on deck with chores and baby care. In the first few weeks you may not get to chores or even a shower some days.

Ask family/friends to help on the hard days.

YOU CAN STILL PLAN YOUR DAY – JUST DIFFERENTLY

Life with a baby may feel unpredictable, but some gentle planning can help you feel more grounded.

- You might choose to sleep when your baby sleeps, especially in the early weeks, to get the rest you need.

- You may find that waking a little earlier helps you feel more organized before the day begins.

- Once baby is awake, it helps to follow their cues: feed when they're hungry, help them sleep when they're tired.

- In the beginning you may just stay home. It takes time for you to get the hang of this new life.

- Once you're ready to go out, aim to plan just one outing or event each day, two at the most and try to work around your baby's sleep cycles.

- Keep some days for staying home. Don't overbook, slow days can be just what both of you need. Connection with you is more important than constant activity. Be wary of overstimulating your baby.

- During naps, you might find a moment to rest, catch up on something you enjoy, or simply breathe.

- Sometimes evenings may offer space for you, if baby settles early, that time can be a gift.

- Let each day unfold, notice what works and what doesn't and give yourself permission to adjust.

- Things like contact naps (when baby sleeps on you) might become sacred moments, your new quiet time, your time to pray or reflect.

WHAT CAN I STILL DO FOR ME?

- Eat well, not just carbs but the rainbow of colours.

- Do some gentle exercise.
- Have some adult conversations.
- Take time out for friends.
- Let others help when they ask.
- Self-care: massage, get your hair done, paint, write your feelings down.
- Breathe, pray, be present, listen to the birds singing.

CARE FOR YOURSELF

Eat **nutritious foods** to stay energized, especially if breastfeeding. Try light exercise and get rest **when baby sleeps**. Prioritize **healing** and go at your own pace. Weight loss is not your priority at this time.

When to See Your Midwife or Doctor

Reach out if you experience:

- Heavy bleeding or clots. The bleeding should slowly decrease over time. If it increases, get yourself reviewed. When breastfeeding it is normal for bleeding to increase slightly after each breastfeed. This is because oxytocin produced during the feed causes the uterus to contract.
- Fever or unpleasant discharge, if you are not sure get yourself checked.
- Painful stitches, breasts, or legs. These should improve each day.

- Low mood that doesn't lift after a couple of weeks.

A **6-week postnatal check** is recommended for physical and emotional wellbeing. If you feel persistently down, know that **postnatal depression is common** and treatable. You're not alone.

Ask yourself are my expectations realistic?

- Are there times when I expect too much of myself and others?
- How can I maintain balance? Let some things go a bit. The house can be messy for a bit.

CHANGING RELATIONSHIPS

Sleep deprivation. It is so hard to not have control over when you can sleep. It is taken out of your hands and depends on your baby's ability to stay calm and sleep. This means you need to make decisions about competing responsibilities. It all feels important but without sleep you will not manage anything well.

Pointers: Sleep when your baby sleeps.

Lack of intimacy: Expect that intimacy will decline after childbirth. This is normal considering the sleep deprivation, new responsibilities and need for the woman's body to heal.

Pointers: Be close and intimate in other ways, such as kissing, touching, snuggling. Make time to physically and emotionally connect with each other.

Responsibilities: The weight of carrying the house and family is substantial.

Pointers: Map out what your routine and responsibilities will look like. Be clear about what will help. Share the load.

If you are finding life hard.

Postnatal depression is real. I believe it sometimes can be prevented by having realistic expectations, planning and good flexible support from people that can hear your heart. Part of writing this book, was in the hope that you can establish support during your pregnancy, so that if you are struggling with the transition of being a mum, you will have those supports around you. We as women need to be heard. Our feelings need to be validated and normalised whether they make sense or not. Feelings don't need to rule our lives; we don't have to sit in those feelings and dwell on them. Someone once told me "You can't stop the birds flying overhead but you can stop them nesting in your hair." Feelings are like the surf; they come and go. There are practical steps that we can take to help us move past them. I remember as the new mum, feeling like my whole world had changed so dramatically, looking at my husband thinking his life hasn't changed that much, he still gets to go out, go to work and have adult conversations, he often still attended his hobbies. I was an enthusiastic Christian and thought somehow that feeling this way was a lack of faith. I kept telling myself that I almost had postnatal depression and did not seek professional help. I wanted a family so much but felt so alone and unsupported. He would come home and say to me "I need to get myself together and wind down before I help you with the children." I had two children fourteen months apart and I was barely holding myself together. He would walk in the door, and I would hand the baby to him. Jack was a really unsettled baby he had many issues that caused him to cry for many hours. Kelsie was only 14 months old when he was born so they were close together in age.

I felt overwhelmed often. I was living in a suburb that was 15 to 20 minutes away from most of my friends and church. They were not available to me. I had my mother-in-law living in the same house as me then in a granny flat at the back of our house. She helped a lot. She was a lovely lady but would often step in and undermine my mothering as I was trying to learn how to respond to cues. I would put Kelsie down to sleep and go to the toilet and I would come out and she would have her up. I'm not telling you this to make you feel sorry for me hopefully you can hear and understand how, when we feel misunderstood, criticized, isolated or ignored the feelings can build up.

I did some work when I was working as a family support worker with mums who had previously had postnatal depression with their first child, and they were pregnant with the second. I would go in and listen to their story. We would talk about why they felt so alone in that early time. We would then work out steps that would help them understand what they can do at what stage if it were to happen again.

<u>Green Light- Step One</u>

Everything's going, okay. You are feeling like you're alright, it's hard adjusting but your family/friends are around when needed and your husband is able to listen and help with the practical steps of caring for your baby and housework. You might have some hard days, but these are balanced out by good days.

<u>Amber Light- Step Two</u>

Things are starting to feel a bit bumpy. You are feeling like you're not managing more often but other times you are still managing. The difference with this stage is there are now more things distressing you, less joy. This was the stage we talked about making more firm plans of help each day. It helps to explore whether you can have some time out for outings. Talking to your husband and Child and Family Health Nurse (if you have one) about how you're feeling. Watch and see whether these things improve the situation.

Bring in your supports more often to help.

<u>Red Light- Step Three</u>

This is the time where each day seems the same. You don't seem to be managing at all. You're spending more time crying. You may not be able to sleep when you do lie down. You feel like nothing is working. You may feel like wanting to run away or that your child would be better off without you, that the world would be better off. These are dangerous thoughts and it's important to seek help (RED FLAG). It's important to have others aware before this stage so they can seek help if you can't.

I suffered with postnatal depression after my second child. I used to say I am almost depressed instead of recognising the signs. I remember one night that was particularly challenging. Jack was crying, I fed him, changed him, I rocked him. Nothing was helping, he would not stop crying and my husband was sleeping peacefully. How did they do that? I thought "I'll give Jack a bath, then the thought occurred to me, if I hold his head underwater, I won't hear him cry" (RED FLAG). Straight away the red flags were waving, and I realised I wasn't in a good space. I gave Jack a bath (keeping his head above the water) and then I woke my husband. I said, "I need some sleep" and he took over. Sleep deprivation is extremely hard to cope with; our brains don't like it. We start to think crazy thoughts. I lived by the railway line and had to cross it regularly. I remember thinking if the train hit me then this would be all over, and I won't have to worry any more (RED FLAG). These thoughts are not good but for me were fleeting and I was not going to act on them. They are more than a concern. I was a midwife and a child and health nurse and there was a lot of pressure I put on myself not to admit that I had postnatal depression. I felt I should be able to cope. I didn't seek help and the depression did impact me for years.

We know that if you seek help early, you will recover much more quickly from postnatal depression. Help doesn't mean that you must take medication. It might be just that you have someone to talk to someone to plan out how to help you in your situation. Some mums choose to self-medicate, in this time, they might start drinking, they might use other drugs. These things just introduce other problems into the mix. It's important to get some help. Postnatal depression is not something to ignore or to minimise and if you're feeling any of these things or even just that it's really hard for you, please seek some help. If you haven't already, talk to your husband/family/friend/GP. It's important for them to know how you are feeling. Sometimes talking about it will help. You made the baby together so need to work at this together. Reach out to them so you can plan some me time. Get them to help with household tasks and baby care.

Depression impacts our ability to talk face to face with our baby, we tend to care for them in an almost robotic fashion. This does not meet their needs for connection. Getting help for you will help your baby too!

Postnatal depression does not mean you have failed. We all need help with this journey.

WHAT CAN HELP?

Spend some time with God each day. He is your most available resource.

Parents, parents in law, and family. Friends with or without children. Friends from work or church. Book a babysitter or get to know your neighbors. Meet with other mums, mother's groups, craft groups, swimming classes, library, online groups. Think about these things in pregnancy writing down somewhere who you can call on. Ask them if they would be available before the baby comes. It is so much easier to call when you have already discussed this. Reach out to Child and Family Health Nurse or phone help lines. Chat to others about how you are feeling.

Body shape

It's hard to imagine why we would expect a body that has carried and birthed a child would look like it did before that. The only thing I can say is social media has made life harder for so many people. Getting back in shape is not a mum's priority when she is learning how to care for another human being. The priority needs to be around rest (when you can), recovery, adjustment, connection and confidence. Relaxin is a hormone that is secreted when you are pregnant. It's job is to soften muscles and ligaments to allow growth and eventual birth of baby. This hormone sticks around after birth in some cases up to 12 months. Its presence means that your muscles and ligaments are not tight like before and too much exercise too soon can mean your back may be at risk of injury. Your body needs to have nutrition and rest. Some gentle exercise when you can, will help your mental health.

Being touched out.

This is an expression I hear more and more. Before birth we welcome close relationships into our personal space for fun and comfort and connection. When we have had enough, we can ask them for space. When we have a baby, we don't have control over when our baby needs to be close. In fact, it's pretty much 24/7! Their needs trump ours most of the time. It might help to put them in the pram and go for a walk when this happens. This is when our village can be a big help. You will eventually adjust to the new you, in many ways you may like the new you better.

FINDING YOUR VALUE IN GOD

Many of us found our value in work or helping others. This is a time in your life where you need to focus on you, your baby and family. Our value is found in who we are and that does not change with time. We are God's creation, created in the image of God. He loves us so much. Our work is raising the next generation. It is undoubtedly the most important work we will ever do.

Recovery Takes time and is different for all of us. Nine months to grow baby and usually nine months to start to feel you again. Looking after baby is hard but don't forget to look after you.

If you were to wake up and things were better how would you know?
WHAT WOULD BE DIFFERENT?

This is something that may help you focus on helpful things to do. What if anything can you do now that may lead to this?

WHAT IF I STILL FEEL DOWN?

- It is important to acknowledge our feelings
- Sometimes there is more going on
- If you have felt down for 2 weeks or more seek help
- Sometimes anxiety is more than normal motherhood adjustment.
- If it is limiting you going out that persists beyond the first few weeks see your GP or seek help from a perinatal support line.

Psalm 46:10
"Be still and know that I am God;
I will be exalted among the nations,
I will be exalted over the earth."

Understanding God's Sovereignty

Recognize that God is in control of all circumstances, and His plans will be fulfilled regardless of human actions.

Practicing Stillness

In a world filled with noise and chaos, intentionally create moments of quiet to focus on God's presence and power.

Trusting in God's Exaltation

Have confidence that God will be glorified among all nations and throughout the earth, regardless of current events.

Responding to Anxiety with Faith

When faced with fear or uncertainty, remember to be still and trust in God's promises and His ultimate authority.

Living with Eternal Perspective

Keep in mind that God's purposes extend beyond our immediate situations, and His glory will be revealed in His timing.

REFERENCES:

Downloaded 26/5/25 and modified from Matrescence: lifetime impact of motherhood on cognition and the brain
Edwina R. Orchard, Helena J.V. Rutherford, Avram J. Holmes ...
January 4, 2023

Help Lines in Australia

COPE www.cope.org
Supporting the mental health of new, hopeful and expectant parents
Centre of Perinatal Excellence (COPE) is Australia's peak body in perinatal mental health.

Forwhen https://forwhenhelpline.org.au
Guiding new and expecting parents to perinatal mental health support

PANDA.org.au. https://www.panda.org.au
PANDA | Support that's always there, for you and your family

Beyond Blue. *https://www.beyondblue.org.au*
Beyond Blue is here to help – whether you're seeking mental health info or free, qualified **support** via chat or phone. Find a life beyond the blues today.

Gidget Foundation. *https://www.gidgetfoundation.org.au*
The Gidget Foundation provides timely, appropriate and specialist *support* for new and expectant parents facing perinatal anxiety and *depression*.

Biblehub insights into Psalm 46:10
https://biblehub.com/study/psalms/46-10.htm

CHAPTER 12
The Fourth Trimester

Isaiah 40:11 (NIV)
"He tends his flock like a shepherd:
He gathers the lambs in his arms and carries them close to his heart;
He gently leads those that have young."

WHAT IS THE FOURTH TRIMESTER?

The fourth trimester is often considered the **first 12 weeks after birth, but I like to say it may go for up to 9 months**. It's a time of huge adjustment for both baby and parents. Your baby is adapting to life outside the womb, and you're adjusting physically and emotionally to parenthood. It's called a "trimester" to emphasize the need to **recreate the comfort of the womb** during this time. Babies don't necessarily need sensory play or any formal form of music therapy. They just need you and time on the floor with you close by. You may need to get out and about and that's ok. I wonder these days if babies are overstimulated with all the activities that they do.

It takes time for your baby to adjust to new surroundings. When we move, we take our familiar things with us, our furniture, our family. It still takes months to feel at home. Your baby's familiar things are your voice, your smell, your heartbeat, movement and your arms holding them.

HELPING YOUR BABY ADJUST

You can ease your newborn's transition with:-

- **Swaddling & Swaying**: Mimics the snug, rhythmic movement of the womb.

- **Skin-to-Skin Contact:** Helps baby feel secure and promotes bonding. Can be done with Dad as well.

- **Feeding Often**: 6–12 times a day, combined with close contact.

- **Warm Baths**: Reminds baby of the womb and encourages relaxation. Babies like a really warm, deep bath. If you feel the water and don't want to get in it's too cold. If it stings its too hot. Put their ears under the water and talk to them. It sounds like it did in the womb.

- **Singing and reading to baby as discussed earlier.**

- **Going for walks. These are great for you and your baby. It's a chance to get out into nature, feel the wind in your hair and listen to the birds sing.**

Dads are so important!

What It Means for Parents:

It's easy to feel **overwhelmed,** exhausted, and overlooked as the focus shifts to baby. Family will walk in and go straight to baby. You're recovering from birth, navigating hormonal changes, and learning a new rhythm. **Support is vital. Please don't try to do it all yourself.** Ask for help, it's **okay** to need help. Support can include meals, chores, baby care, or watching other children. If you have a partner, share responsibilities early and openly. Remember to talk to Jesus all day, especially for guidance. Give Him praise for this journey even when you don't feel like it.

THIS WORK MATTERS DEEPLY

Caring for a baby is big. It's both emotionally and physically exhausting. It takes time to grow into the role and feel confident in it. This is your first true 24/7 role and it's often said to be the equivalent of *two* full-time jobs. How you respond to your baby's cues shapes their brain and sets the foundation for lifelong mental health. They'll grow up knowing they have value. They'll grow up knowing they are loved. And none of this is easy, it's not for the faint-hearted. But you're not doing it alone. God is with you in the quiet, the chaos, and everything in between. God is with you every step of the way.

Isaiah 30:21
Your ears shall hear a word behind you, saying,
"This is the way, walk in it,
Whenever you turn to the right hand or
whenever you turn to the left."

I am sure you have felt I have repeated myself a bit during this book. I am passionate about you getting the right support. You will be the best mother for this child God has given you. You won't be perfect none of us are.

Safety of Abiding in the Presence of God PSALM 91

91 He who dwells in the secret place of the Most High
Shall abide under the shadow of the Almighty.
2 I will say of the Lord, "He is my refuge and my fortress;
My God, in Him I will trust."
3 Surely He shall deliver you from the snare of the [a]fowler
And from the perilous pestilence.
4 He shall cover you with His feathers,
And under His wings you shall take refuge;
His truth shall be your shield and [b]buckler.
5 You shall not be afraid of the terror by night,
Nor of the arrow that flies by day,
6 Nor of the pestilence that walks in darkness,
Nor of the destruction that lays waste at noonday.
7 A thousand may fall at your side,
And ten thousand at your right hand;
But it shall not come near you.
8 Only with your eyes shall you look,
And see the reward of the wicked.
9 Because you have made the Lord, who is my refuge,
Even the Most High, your dwelling place,
10 No evil shall befall you,
Nor shall any plague come near your dwelling;
11 For He shall give His angels charge over you,
To keep you in all your ways.
12 In their hands they shall [c]bear you up,
Lest you [d]dash your foot against a stone.
13 You shall tread upon the lion and the cobra,
The young lion and the serpent you shall trample underfoot.
14 "Because he has set his love upon Me, therefore I will deliver him;
I will [e]set him on high, because he has known My name.
15 He shall call upon Me, and I will answer him;
I will be with him in trouble;
I will deliver him and honor him.
16 With [f]long life I will satisfy him,
And show him My salvation."

When we sit at Jesus' feet we bring pleasure to our God. He loves our company. There is no greater thing we can do, even greater than our role as mother. All else fades. He is worthy of our praise. Our Magnificent God wants you to know this calling, this motherhood, is your worship to Him. Walk and talk together often, walk in humility giving Him the Glory.

I found this helpful to do at the end of the day. This is a version of the five-step Daily Examen that St. Ignatius practiced. It may be as short as 5 mins if you are pushed for time.

The Prayer of Examen https://fullerstudio.fuller.edu/prayer-of-examen/

The Prayer of Examen is a spiritual practice of reviewing the day to retune ourselves to the sacred in ordinary life. Usually lasting 15–20 minutes and done in the evening, the prayer prompts us to remember God's presence, express gratitude, reflect on the day, and prepare for the day to come.

1. Ask God for Light

Stop, breathe deeply, and know that you are in God's presence. God has been with you since the beginning of your day, in every detail. As you prepare to look back on your day, ask the Holy Spirit to shine the light that will clear your vision—so you might see what God wants you to see.

Psalm 139:7-8

"Where could I go to get away from your spirit? Where could I go to escape your presence? If I went up to heaven, you would be there. If I went down to the grave, you would be there too!"

2. Give Thanks

Every moment in your day is a gift from God. Be thankful for all of it, even the smallest things: a patch of blue sky, the music in your headphones, a smile from a stranger. Allow gratitude to draw you into the fullness of your life.

> *Psalm 9:1-2*
> *"I will thank you, Lord, with all my heart; I will talk about all your wonderful acts. I will celebrate and rejoice in you; I will sing praises to your name, Most High."*

3. Review the Day

Think back over your day: who you were with, where you were, what you did—however ordinary. Recall the sights, sounds, smells, conversations, thoughts, and feelings you experienced. What enlivened you? What discouraged you? Give your attention to those moments and offer them to God.

> *Psalm 139 1-3*
> *"Lord, you have examined me. You know me. You know when I sit down and when I stand up. Even from far away, you comprehend my plans. You study my traveling and resting. You are thoroughly familiar with all my ways."*

4. Face Your Shortcomings

As you consider your day, reflect honestly on the moments you felt out of tune with God—something you said, a missed opportunity, some way you wish you had acted differently. For what do you need forgiveness? Do you need to make things right with someone else? Look at your shortcomings and allow God to heal them.

Psalm 51:10-12:
"Create in me a clean heart, O God, and put a new and right spirit within me. Do not cast me away from your presence, and do not take your holy spirit from me. Restore to me the joy of your salvation and sustain in me a willing spirit."

5. Look Toward the Day to Come

As you end your day, look to tomorrow. What are you looking forward to, and what concerns you? Ask for God's help in the future: to open your eyes, your ears, and your heart to see where God is working. Remember that God will again be present tomorrow in all things large and small, guiding you toward fullness in your life.

Psalm 121: 1,2,8
"I raise my eyes toward the mountains. Where will my help come from? My help comes from the Lord, the maker of heaven and earth. The Lord will protect you on your journeys whether going or coming from now until forever from now."

The Prayer of Examen on this website offers video footage to help you to do this if you are more visual in your learning.

Let me finish with a prayer

> **Dear Lord Jesus**
>
> *You are so amazing! Thank you for all you do. Help each of us to connect with you more and listen to Your whispers. Help each mother reading this book to feel confident in what You have given them to do, this wonderful job of mothering.*
>
> *I thank you for the comfort, direction, inspiration, protection and provision you provide. I pray that this beautiful woman will know her worth as a child of the mighty King.*
>
> **In Jesus Mighty Name**
>
> **Amen**

I am happy for you to connect with me on facebook or Instagram.
Look for Learning the Baby Dance or just Jenni Helm
If you need breastfeeding support or birth debriefing I can do this virtually.
www.learningthebabydance.com.au

www.ingramcontent.com/pod-product-compliance
Lightning Source LLC
LaVergne TN
LVHW051122080426
835510LV00018B/2183